D1636800

BECOMING A
BARBARIAN

JACK DONOVAN

DISSONANT HUM

CASCADIA

First Paperback Edition.

ISBN-13: 978-0-9854523-5-3

Cover and Interior Artwork and Design by Jack Donovan.

Published by Jack Donovan.

[DH]

[DISSONANT HUM]
4230 SE King Road, No. 185
Milwaukie, Oregon. 97222
USA.

www.dissonant-hum.com

Subjects:
1. Social Sciences - Men's Studies
2. Psychology - Men
4. Men - Social Conditions
5. Philosophy
6. Gender Studies

CONTENTS

PREFACE

In some crass and crooked form, tribalism has become a trendy marketing buzzword, a cute and superficial synonym for "loyal customer."

However, true tribalism — a commitment to one group of people above and potentially at the expense of all others — remains deeply taboo. Tribalism remains the bane of the United Nations and the boogeyman of humanity-huggers, peaceniks and one-worlders throughout the West.

Even the mainstream, controlled opposition political parties are routinely chastised for their tame tribal attitudes. One must never cheer too loudly or fight too hard. It's all game, and you have to be able to hug it out after the final scores are tallied. Even war is just "winning hearts and minds."

The Way of Men — my book about masculinity, meant to be read before reading this book — concluded by suggesting that men who wanted to live masculine lives and who want to be surrounded by men who share their values should go out and build a "gang." It was implied that from the gang, men would build tribes, following the semi-mythical model of the early Romans. In my essay "The Brotherhood," in *A Sky Without Eagles*, I elaborated on the importance of building family and an ancestor cult into the tribal brotherhood.

I try to do the things I tell my readers to do, to the best of my ability. I told them to go out and join a gang or tribe, so I went out and joined a tribe. I patched into a heathen tribe known as The Wolves of Vinland in June 2015, after nearly a year of prospecting. Since then, I've been building my own *Männerbund* here in Cascadia. I've learned many lessons about tribalism and leadership since then, and I'm sure I'll learn a lot more. I expect these lessons to inform whatever I write in the future.

Men always ask me for a guide to actually building a tribe. Ask me again in ten years, or maybe twenty, and I'll let you know how it all worked out.

But what became clear to me as I started talking to men about the idea of starting or joining a tribe is that most Western men are hesitant to allow themselves to think tribally.

Western men, especially white Western men — though many men from other backgrounds have absorbed some of the same ideas — don't know how to become the kind men who could become a member of a tribe. This is a fairly recent development, as it wasn't so long ago that Europeans were able to put aside their similarities and fight each other to the death over matters of religion or national honor. The same has always been true of the peoples of Asia and Africa and Central America.

Today, all good, modern, civilized men living in the Western world are all taught to be good global citizens whose racial, cultural and religious loyalties must always be subordinate to a broader and more inclusive commitment to the human race. To say that you care about one group of people more than others is a moral sin in the modern world. It is considered uncivilized — barbaric.

And yet, to become the kind of man who can join or start a tribe, that is exactly what you have to be willing to do. You have to be willing to become an outsider — a barbarian — to the rest of the world.

The first half of this book explores this conflict between masculinity and tribalism and identity and modern Western civilization, or "The Empire of Nothing." The second half of the book explores some of the changes of the mind that men will have to make if they want to become the kind of men who could truly live tribally, beyond the psychological boundaries of the Empire — as barbarians.

Because I have become a barbarian, I make no apologies for framing some chapters and arguments with the culture of my own tribe, which is oriented to some extent around Germanic lore. Whether that culture appeals to you or not, I believe the basic concepts discussed could be applicable to tribes drawing inspiration from a wide variety of other cultural, religous and ethnic backgrounds.

START THE WORLD!

Jack Donovan
Cascadia Bioregion
February, 2016.

THE FATE OF MEN

Masculinity is tragic.

Masculinity is a lifelong struggle, a gauntlet run against nature and other men to demonstrate virility and prove one's worthiness as a man in the eyes of other men. Masculinity is a challenge to honor that ends only in death — a challenge to win coupled with a guarantee that, eventually, even the best men will lose.

Masculinity means being born a boy who can only become a man by becoming stronger, by overcoming fearfulness, by becoming more competent and confident in his abilities, and by earning the respect and admiration of other males.

Every boy is born cursed. Every boy will be tried and measured against others and he soon perceives or understands instinctively — he soon knows that the way of men is the way of competition and strife. The way to manhood is through the gauntlet, and there is no end to it. Manhood is not a destination but a title to be defended.

The idea that a man should be "secure in his masculinity" is a bourgeois fantasy invented by therapists and repeated by women. Every king, every chief, every world record holder and every silverback gorilla looks over his shoulder. Being good at being a man just means the challenges get dialed up and the challengers become more formidable.

This gauntlet must be run whether a boy likes it or not, whether he accepts it or rejects it. To reject the struggle is forfeiture. Avoiding the struggle is an acceptance of defeat and a demonstration of spiritual cowardice.

There are some who will applaud this kind of forfeiture as if it were courageous, but they are despisers of masculinity and strength. They are foolish women or failed men or deceitful manipulators who prefer men to be passive, for reasons of their own.

However, accepting the fate of men and running the gauntlet of manliness means understanding that the fight is never truly fair, and that all men are not born with the same strengths.

Accepting the fate of men also means understanding that the fight is rigged, and that every man will either die early or live to see himself decline. Every man who does not die in his prime will live to see his body fail and become weaker, making him more reticent. Most men will live to see their father's competence falter, then their own competence falter, and they will live to see themselves lose the esteem of men. The best an older man can hope for is to have his achievements remembered, and to be respected for his wisdom and consulted for his experience.

Understanding masculinity means understanding that men can only reach their greatest potential through vital conflict and competition with other men. The way of men is the way of the pack hunt, and man is the most dangerous game. Human masculinity is the evolutionary product of gang selection — of bands of men who hunted and fought their way through far more perilous and demanding ages. Human masculinity — the testing and proving of strength, courage, mastery and the desire to earn the respect of a given group of men — requires conflict to thrive, but also to survive.

Eternal peace is the death of manliness. The peace sign is a death rune.

Strength can only be tested against resistance and courage can only be tested through risk. Competence matters most when it is most desperately needed.

Honor requires an honor group — a finite group of men to stand in judgement of each other's virtues. No man can prove himself to every man, everywhere, and the expectation that men should have to prove themselves to every man and woman creates a sense of futility. If the number of judges and challengers is infinite, why bother? If every man is both a brother and a potential threat, who do you fight for? Who do you become the strongest and most courageous and most competent version of yourself *for*? How much can any one man's honor matter when he must answer to and be compared to billions of other men, of other strangers who do not and cannot care what he does or how he lives or whether he lives or dies? A man and his honor get lost among the numberless hordes. Because a man cannot be accountable to everyone, without an honor group — without a tribe — he is accountable only to his own ego. A man without a *Männerbund* can flatter himself freely and he will be more likely than others would be to accept his own excuses. Most religions defer the final assessment of a man's deeds to the gods, but the judgment of the gods is far-too-conveniently post-mortem. Brothers judge you to your face, in the here and now.

This phenomenon of masculinity is a human universal. Men all around the world and throughout history have shared the fate of men. In every dominant culture known, men have pushed each other to be stronger, more courageous and more competent. They have tested each other and shamed or expelled men who refused to be tested, who made them look weaker as a group. Manhood has always been demanding, it has always been a trail that ends only in death, and it has always been tragic.

To compound the tragedy of manhood, masculinity is a human universal — something that all men have in common — but universalism destroys masculinity. Without separation there can be no conflict and without conflict there can be no vital masculinity. To say that you love every man as your brother is not only a *lie*, but a resignation to impotence and a forfeiture of manhood.

It has been said that many enemies bring much honor, and it is also true that without enemies, there can be no honor. Without outsiders, there can be no insiders. Without "them," there can be no "us." Without "us," there can be no honor group, and therefore, no honor.

The experience of being a man is something all men have in common, an experience shared and understood by friends and enemies alike, but the very nature of masculinity demands that we go to our corners and fight it out.

This drive to conflict is the fate of men.

It is tragic, but all life is tragic.

We live, but are destined to die.

All of our life stories are a collection of highs and lows, of victories and defeats, of struggles and of overcoming. Without conflict, no life story is worth telling. Without conflict and struggle, the answer to the question "What happened?" is: "Nothing."

Like Odin and Thor, we know we will die, but unless we fight, we are already as good as dead.

Better to live vigorously, better to fight, than to simply wait for the end...in peace.

Ber er hver að baki nema sér bróður eigi.
"Bare is the back of a brotherless man."

— Njal's Saga

IDENTITY IS EVERYTHING

It has always been the way of men to identify a group of friends, allies and kin, to draw a perimeter around them, to fight to protect them and to advance their interests.

The absence of social identity — of belonging to any clearly defined group — conjures the Hobbesian fantasy of the warre of "all against all" where men are friendless and every man and woman and child is a potential enemy. This friendless, low-trust world is chaotic, inhuman and temporary.

One could imagine it cinematically in some kind of sci-fi prison planet where strangers from different worlds who speak different languages are dropped off to fend for themselves. Or perhaps in the aftermath of disaster in a cosmopolitan city where displaced commuters struggle to survive among strangers.

But you know how that story goes. Even if they have to use improvised sign language, people will seek out alliances. The weak will seek protection. The strong will seek out fellow guardians to help them survive, and to protect and expand their assets, charges and dependents. These alliances bring a sense of order and direction to chaos and disorientation.

Order demands violence, but the drive to order is the product of identity. Whether it is a matter of "us" deciding how to proceed or "us" deciding how to control "them," order cannot be established or maintained without collective coercive actions. Ordered violence is violence coordinated by allies — the opposite of the chaotic melee of every man fighting against every man.

These alliances are the root of collective identity, and over time any group of "us" will develop its own internal culture — at first maybe just a collection of mutually understood jokes, collective memories, shared stories, and recognition of similar preferences. Over time and with some human creativity, these exchanges can develop into a rich and completely distinct cultural identity. These cultures are the product of separateness and discrimination. They can only flourish and be maintained so long as the boundaries between insiders and outsiders are observed and preserved.

Men who have no collective identity — who have no strong alliances or sense of belonging in a particular ingroup — are wanderers dependent on a larger system that rules from above. Humans are social animals. The loner who wants to be alone is an anomalous deviation — however romantic the brooding archetype of the wandering individualist may be. The loner is essentially missing half of his identity. He has no orientation, no context.

This free-floating state of chaos makes humans nervous, so they frantically adopt symbols that identify them with some group of people — however superficial, transient or inconsequential that group may in fact be. This desperation is exploited by bourgeois consumer culture, which encourages people to identify and arrange themselves according to their entertainment preferences, hobbies or other purchase patterns.

Consumer identities are disposable, superficial and subject to changes in fashion or circumstances. Ultimately, they prove unsatisfying, because an identity that can be easily shrugged off or replaced, or which can coexist with competing or conflicting identities fails to stabilize the self-image after its initial novelty has worn off. This creates an endless restlessness that drives the market for new consumer identities and more loose affiliations. These lightweight, shifting connections always leave enough emptiness for that nagging, navel-gazing question pondered by the lonely, spoiled cosmopolitan mind:

"Who am I?"

A man who has earned his place in a group of men knows who he is. A man who knows who his "we" is doesn't have to wonder "who he is." He doesn't have to meditate on every dendrite of his own spiritual snowflake to "find himself." He doesn't have to find himself because he knows where he belongs. His personal identity is located within and relates to his social identity. His idea of himself is not a daydream or a whim, it is repeatedly verified and peer-reviewed. His ego is balanced by his superego.

Imagine the amusement of backwoods tribesman and villagers when confronted with frivolous, deracinated Westerners who have travelled to South America or the Far East searching for "enlightenment" or "meaning."

Social identity *is* meaning. It is the "why" that follows naturally from the "we." Without a firm social context, humans are disoriented and actions become relatively arbitrary and meaningless. Social identity is social orientation. It is the starting point from which the spear extends.

Identity is a rootedness that provides a rationale for action.

UNIVERSAL IMPOTENCE

If tribal identity is everything that matters, then, in the absence of tribal identity, nothing really matters. There is only chaos and disorientation, confusion and anxiety, arbitrariness of action and a rootless emptiness.

Modern Western governments and corporations — a synergistic collaboration of independently operating international self-interested entities which I'll collectively call "The Empire of Nothing" — are concerned primarily with facilitating global trade, so it is pragmatic for them to encourage moral universalism. By moral universalism, I mean applying the same moral principles to everyone, everywhere and treating everyone as part of the same ingroup.

It is in the interest of the Empire to discourage exclusive identity, tribalism, and even nationalism to whatever extent it is practical within a given area, with a given group, at a given time. Well-established Western people are expected to open their arms wider than displaced, disenfranchised and decidedly more tribal minorities to welcome them to the global fold and help them to assimilate to the lifestyles of the Western consumer society.

Any vestigial sense of social identity still present in Western men, any desire to observe and maintain social boundaries or protect perimeters, is highly discouraged by Western governments and corporate cultures alike. Racial identity, religious identity, nationalism and even sexual identity are becoming increasingly taboo among Western white men. Good, modern, civilized white men are expected to purge from their hearts and minds any trace of natural human tribalism that might prevent any people from feeling uncomfortable within the Empire.

Despite the heavy-handed subterfuges of "multiculturalism" and "diversity is our strength," the underlying reality is that within a few generations, any living culture will dissolve into an innocuous and half-remembered "cultural heritage" and the descendants of separate and even intransigent groups will become interchangeable consumers, voters and employees. If they don't, they'll end up prisoners, and that also suits the Empire of Nothing.

While this process is underway...good, modern, civilized men are asked to think of themselves not as citizens of nations, but as "citizens of the world."

Good, modern, civilized men are not supposed to care about their people because *everyone* is supposed to be "their people."

Good, modern, civilized men are expected to care about all of humanity.

They are supposed to care about everyone's happiness and protect everyone from suffering and injustice.

Good, modern, civilized men are burdened with the expectation that they must somehow become the guardians of all and none.

7.2 billion struggling souls...and we're expected to care about the fate of all of them — but none too much.

To any man's mind, even one billion people might as well be an infinite number of people. The human mind cannot meaningfully conceptualize that many upright monkeys. It's just a number. If you started writing down the names of these people — which are nearly meaningless tags for entire lifetimes of human thought and experience — at an average rate of 6 seconds per name, without breaks or sleep, it would take you 190 years or so to write down one billion names. You wouldn't know anything about those people, you wouldn't remember more than a few of those names, and you would have lived and died at least twice in the diabolical torture chamber where you were assigned this task. And of course, many will have died and been born during that time. The world population is projected to be 9.6 billion by 2050, based on current growth rates. By then, you poor tormented bastard, you will only have written down a completely inadequate 178 million names or so.

What it actually means to care about everyone on the planet is so far beyond the processing power of the human brain that you might as well be talking about perceiving eternity or infinite space or any other concept we can really only talk about in completely abstract and theoretical terms.

To perceive oneself in the context of billions of people, and I imagine this is a guilty pleasure especially among elites and others who think very highly of themselves, you must step back and over the world and see people as mere trends, percentages, swarms of microscopic organisms invisible to the naked eye.

If you prefer to despair, attempt to imagine yourself and the meaning of your life in the context of just a billion people and caring about them all equally. It is as disorienting as floating alone in space. Universal humanity is so much of something that it's nothing. Placing yourself among billions is like setting your soul adrift in the void.

To be one with billions isn't "enlightenment," it's self-negation. It's inhuman.

Total unity is total death.

Now it will be argued that no one is actually expected to care that much about people they've never met, and that one should focus on treating the people one actually encounters in everyday life with a universal morality. This is closer to the scale of human life and would make a lot more sense to our ancestors, who for a long time weren't even sure about the shape of the planet much less the number of people on it or what was going on 3,000 or even 300 miles away.

However, this argument is undermined by the aims of many social justice movements — or swarms of stupid microorganisms, if you prefer — which work to impose globalist values and moral universalism and whichever "human rights" they've made up on people they've never met. It is also undermined by international organizations and by the farcical moral rationales offered for wars overseas.

"We can't let these people you've never met oppress these other people you've never met in the Middle East or Vietnam or wherever... because 'human rights.'"

"You should go fight to the death to fix that for "truth" or "justice" or....something."

But, for the sake of argument, let's say you are a good, modern, civilized man who is fully invested in the globalist project of eradicating social injustice, racism, sexism, classism. You're committed to treating every other human like family. You're going to apply functional tribal ideals, like The Golden Rule, to everyone you meet. You're going to assume that everyone is innocent until proven guilty, and you are going to treat them as you'd want to be treated. You're going to ignore stereotypes — which are informational profiles of groups of people that may or may not be accurate at the individual level — and treat everyone else as if they are in your group and have the same basic "human" values.

This moral universalism makes men weak, vulnerable and stupid.

Researchers say that the human brain can only maintain meaningful relationships with about 150-250 people at a given time, depending on what kind of relationship you consider meaningful. You can't possibly know more people than that well enough to trust them. Everyone else is a stranger. Now, within a homogenous cultural group where social codes and values are normalized, you can probably afford to treat most people the way you'd want to be treated, because they are theoretically playing by the same rules. However it still makes good sense to be careful when you deal with strangers, and if your mother cared about you at all, she already taught you that.

However, in a pluralistic or multicultural zone where there are many people from many groups, many of whom have different values, codes and loyalties, there is a far higher likelihood that your generous assumption will be wrong. You can choose to believe that everyone really wants peace and harmony, or that people all just really want to get along and follow the rules, but your belief would be wrong. Choosing to believe something doesn't make it true.

Tactically speaking, it makes far more sense to make assumptions about how people will behave based on in-group social signalling and other cues.

It makes perfect sense to assume that a black man on the sidewalk who is outfitted like the stereotype of an urban street thug will act like an urban street thug. He's signalling ingroup affiliation and identifying himself with urban street thugs. If he was wearing a cardigan sweater with a button-up shirt sitting in a college classroom, you might not worry as much. You might be wrong about either one, but based on the information available, the odds are in your favor.

Avoiding a potential security threat by assuming the black man dressed as a thug is a potential attacker is just as rational as walking into a rural watering hole and making the reasonable assumption that the redneck contingent mean-mugging you really *doesn't* like the look of you. Your peaceful intentions don't make you a member of their in-group, and they may not care about your intentions at all. They may decide to harass you for sport, out of sheer boredom.

Part of the purpose of wearing religious garb is to identify members and separate them from strangers. When someone wears special headgear or a special outfit for their religion, part of what they are doing is signalling that they are part of another group, a subculture within or separate from your group. They are sending a message that they have different values from you and that they care about enough adhering to the codes of their ingroup and maintaining a boundary between insiders and outsiders that they are willing to risk your suspicion. They are loyal to a group and proud to be part of it. They're saying "I'm not on your team," or at the very least, "I'm on this other team, first."

Yet, in pluralistic Western democracies, men are taught that is morally wrong to judge a book by its cover. Men are taught that it is wrong to make snap judgements and that they should assume the best case scenario instead of making decisions based on the worst case scenario. Even when someone says outright in plain language that they are not on your team and are actually working against you, you will be warned about jumping to conclusions and stereotyping.

Many white Western men and women are so committed to moral universalism that no matter what people from other groups say or do, instead of taking it at face value, they attempt to downplay it or explain it away or even take the blame for it.

"Fuck Whitey"

We should listen to what he has to say and try to understand his experience.

"Fuck the Police"

He's probably responding to unfair racial profiling and economic injustice.

"Allahu Akbar!" [BOOM!]

Perhaps we've offended him.

No matter what information they're presented with, many Westerners have become so mincingly deferential, so committed to the limp-dick Lennon-ist pipe dream that the whole "world should live as one," so burdened by their inherited white guilt that they'll put anyone and everyone else's interests before their own — that they refuse to accurately evaluate the information presented to them.

In practice, moral universalism — often perversely called "humanism" — has become a secular catechism of self-denial and spiritual surrender. Like religious penitents, universalists flail and torment themselves for even having improper or unkind thoughts about their fellow human beings. And like inquisitors, their righteousness drives them to rout or ruin any heretic who dares to speak his sinful thoughts aloud.

Negative information about immigrants and minority groups is covered up by egalitarians or so legally perilous to talk about in some parts of the West that the polite and well-meaning nation of Sweden has become known as the rape capital of Europe. Instead of dealing with the problem, the Swedes obscure and talk around it and many have simply accepted it as the "new normal."

Self-defense and firearms instructors often talk about a dynamic decision making process called the OODA Loop. It's a loop people work through to make all kinds of decisions, but it is especially helpful to think about it when examining tactical approaches to fighting scenarios. OODA is an acronym that stands for Observe, Orient, Decide and Act.

Success in a given situation depends on observing it as clearly and accurately as possible, orienting yourself within that situation, making a decision about how to proceed based on that data, executing that plan, and then returning to the beginning of the loop to re-assess the situation as it unfolds.

You could imagine this in terms of a large battle, but also at the scale and speed of a fistfight. If you give someone false information — if you throw out a feint or fake, and then come at your opponent from a different direction — you may be able to land a punch because you've influenced his OODA loop to your advantage. If he opens himself up for a strike, it will be because he failed to assess your intentions accurately, and made a poor decision about how to act.

If a man held up his fist and said he was going to punch you, and you simply refused to believe it, your belief alone wouldn't change his intent. If he decided to punch you, your belief alone wouldn't prevent his fist from hitting your face.

Anyone watching would think you were either blind or dumb for being unable to accurately observe the unfolding circumstances and the information being provided to you.

However, the real problem was in your orientation — in your belief about how the world works and your place in it. Because you believed the man would not hit you, you made the decision not to act, and relied on your mistaken belief instead of protecting yourself.

Refusing to interpret threats or any information accurately because you don't *want* to believe it is obviously foolish.

But Western men are expected to act like fools.

They have abandoned their social identities, and therefore have no social orientation in the world. Or, rather, they are oriented against orientation. The only thing they stand against is identity. Identity is everything, so essentially they've become the champions of nothingness.

Good, modern, civilized white men stand for nothing, so as the saying goes, they'll fall for anything.

And they've been so easily manipulated.

Good, modern, civilized Western white men are so easily cowed by charges of bias and privilege that they work tirelessly to outdo each other with social displays of moral universalism — by cucking themselves in every way imaginable.

Western men are supposed to ignore all negative information about other "underprivileged" groups and behave as if everything is fine whether it is or not. They are expected to let other groups do whatever they want and smile and pretend everything is getting better. Anyone from any group can move to their neighborhoods, and if crime and graffiti and property damage increase, then good, modern, civilized Western men are supposed to make up some abstract and conveniently impossible to prove rationale for why it is happening instead of holding the group in question accountable.

Anyone from any group — but usually self-hating white intellectuals and professors and entertainment industry whores — can slander the ancestors of white men and rewrite their history and all good, modern, civilized white men are supposed to agree and apologize and beg for forgiveness. Even rape is reduced to an economic exchange, where the rapist is excused because of his poverty.

To make sure that women, who are actually a majority group in most populations, feel comfortable and affirmed and safe enough to be good employees and voters and consumers in the Empire, Western men are supposed to constantly ask women for permission and make sure women don't feel threatened or undermined in any way.

When Western men recognize that they have an advantage or someone accuses one of them of some real or imagined "privilege," they're expected to acknowledge it and step aside or handicap themselves in some perverse Harrison Bergeron fashion to make things more "equal" and "fair" for everyone else — as if life has ever been or ever could be fair, as if people had ever been or could be truly equal.

Good, modern, civilized Western white men are expected to be the gentlemen of the world, throwing their coats down and opening every door for everyone else, putting their own interests last.

No one — certainly no woman — respects a man who behaves like that.

No child respects a father like that.

No one respects a man who is always apologizing and backpedaling.

No one respects a man who is always asking for permission.

No one respects a man who won't stand up for himself or fight for his own interests.

No one wants to cheer for a team that stopped playing to win.

Most people would agree that men who don't play to win deserve to lose.

I agree completely.

Moral universalism is a philosophy for men who have surrendered. They have surrendered their land, their history, their women, their dignity and their identity. They've become impotent half-men who deserve to be victims and slaves.

Moral universalism is a poisonous, emasculating philosophy for any man who adopts it.

If you are not a Western white man, and you adopt this philosophy, you will also eventually lose your culture and your history and your identity and you will also deserve to be a victim and a slave. Your cappuccino-colored kin will disappear completely into that incomprehensible swarm of 9.5 billion indistinguishable cappuccino-colored drones.

They may have come for our identities first, but eventually, they'll come for yours.

The interests and mechanisms that drive the Empire have no use for identity. Identity is an inconvenience. It's inefficient. It's in the way.

The forces of globalism are aligned against identity, against everything that means anything.

Together, they form an Empire of Nothing.

THE EMPIRE OF NOTHING

The Empire of Nothing has no Emperor.

The Romans had what could be called an Empire by every other criteria before they had an Emperor. But throughout their expansion, emanating from the center of the Empire, there was Rome and Roman culture. There was the Roman pantheon of gods, there were Roman cults and rituals, there was an acknowledgement that conquered territories were being ruled by Roman families — a patrician class that claimed a lineage going all the way back to the founding of the city.

The Roman Empire maintained a powerful, centralized cultural identity during its most successful centuries and imposed this cultural hegemony on all of its territories. Conquered people knew they were being ruled by Romans, and they were generally required to observe Roman holidays and pay homage to the Roman gods — who, one must have imagined, bestowed great power on the Romans who honored them. Most of the new Roman subjects were polytheists anyway, and they were permitted to worship their old gods so long as they also worshipped the Roman gods.

It is often said that the problem the Romans had with Christians was that they refused to worship the Roman gods. Essentially, they refused to accept Roman identity. Christians wanted to maintain their own identity, and it was everything to them. The Romans knew that identity was everything, that social order was the product of shared identity, and that tolerating the rejection of their centralized, homogenizing identity would be inviting a slow rot to gnaw away at everything they created and cared about. So they persecuted the Christians, though apparently they did so with insufficient vigor.

Other Empires, whether they had an Emperor by name, or a pharaoh, or a great chief, or a King or Queen, maintained a centralized cultural hegemony throughout their acquired territories. Conquered people knew who ruled them. The power came from one place and was the heritage of one culturally unified group of people. It had an origin, and in most cases had a face. Subjects knew what gods they were encouraged or expected to worship, and what customs they'd have to adopt if they didn't want to have a bad time.

The Empire of Nothing has no Emperor, no center and no people.

One might say that the cultural center of the Empire of Nothing is Los Angeles, and they'd be partially correct. In fact the Hollywood entertainment industry illustrates the mechanism and values of the Empire reasonably well. The culture produced is produced primarily for profit. Films and television shows are tested with audiences to assure the broadest appeal and the highest profit. The content produced may appeal to some more than others, but it can never be overtly exclusive. Everything must be for everyone, and no one too much. The most successful and celebrated entertainment products have "universal appeal." It is sometimes said that this is cultural hegemony, but it is entirely market-driven. If Mormons became the most powerful and populous economic group in the nation, and they were known to be avid movie-goers, there would be more big budget Mormon-themed movies. As demographics in America have changed, the big studios have rushed to include actors that reflect those demographics. There is no cultural hegemony emanating from a particular people with a particular identity, merely a profit-driven system of production that responds to changes in the market, with the aim of reaching the most consumers possible. The only culture being imposed through this mechanism is anti-culture — moral and cultural universalism that dissolves social boundaries to make the maximum number of consumers feel included.

While a great deal of cultural product is generated in Los Angeles, Hollywood is not Rome. The "People of Los Angeles" are not imposing their culture on the world. If they even had a culture, it would be the inherited ethic of the sensationalistic and low-pandering vaudeville performers and producers who became some of the first big names in the film industry.

The anticulture of the Empire of Nothing is passively imposed through the Hollywood spectacle — a modern Circus Maximus — but it is actively imposed by government institutions. The governments which impose it are not only based in Washington, D.C., but also throughout the capitals of Europe and particularly in Belgium and New York City. The United Nations and the European Union align against identity wherever it becomes too powerful or threatens to destabilize economies or redraw existing borders. Hollywood shows images of people from different groups living and working together in peace and harmony, but it is governments, institutions and international organizations that punish them when they don't.

Corporations also punish and penalize people for "discrimination" in the workplace, which is acting to protect exclusionary identities or enforce a non-universalistic moral code. In many cases, corporations and ambitious lawyers have been far ahead of states in terms of enforcing racial, sexual and cultural integration around the world. Along with universities, they pioneered the everyday implementation of "diversity" and "cultural sensitivity" training.

Corporations are often portrayed as evil groups of greedy men plotting against minority interests, but in reality the publicly traded corporation is simply an amoral, profit-driven legal entity that sees everything in terms of its bottom line. People are simply consumers and employees. Employees aren't people, they are animated skill sets which perform functions. When it is profitable to replace people with computers that reproduce their functions, they will be replaced. Automatic teller and self-checkout machines are an example encountered every day, but examples in manufacturing and other industries are endless. As a legal entity, a publicly traded corporation has no loyalty to a particular people or nation. When it is profitable, that entity will import people with a given skill set who will work for the lowest salary, or open up a division in a different country if the people there have the skills and will work cheaply enough.

Antagonistic identities are disruptive to the work environment. People who are supposed to be working together can't be members of warring tribes who are always at each other's throats. You're not going to increase collective productivity by telling your co-worker that she's going to Hell, or should be at home in the kitchen, or that her religion is stupid, or that her people are boy-raping goat-fuckers. The corporation benefits from taking the Roman approach. Employees are allowed to maintain their cultural identities at a superficial, non-disruptive level, so long as they bend a knee to the superordinate corporate culture and its goals.

Today's effective human resources manager explains, in comforting and motherly tones…

"Susan, you can wear a cross necklace; Mohammed, you can take as many prayer breaks as you need as long as you get your work done; and Steven, you can dress like a woman — as long as you all agree to be polite to each other and worship Apple Computers."

For some, what I'm calling The Empire of Nothing may invite comparisons to conspiracy theorists obsessing about the New World Order or the Freemasons or the Illuminati or the Bilderberg Group or the Cathedral or the spectacle or, in the most daring and typically the most anonymous of circles, "International Jewry." While certain groups and individuals absolutely do exert more influence over the direction of things than others, I'm hesitant to look for something as conveniently comic-book as a shadowy cabal of villains who rule the world in secret.

It is *possible* that the Reptilians are behind all of this.

But then it would rightly be called The Great Reptilian Empire, and that would be an Empire of Something. Once the Reptilians revealed themselves to us, after a few revolts and skirmishes, we'd all bend a knee to The Green One — whose true name is likely unspeakable — and if the Reptilians were as smart as the Romans were they'd let us pledge our allegiance to The Green One but continue to worship our silly earth gods and smoke pot and play video games and jerk off to dwarf and donkey porn while they harvested a tasteful percentage of our resources or souls or whatever it is that they want.

This is...*possible*.

However, the reality of our plight is probably far more mundane.

The Empire of Nothing is an international collection of self-interested and self-perpetuating systems with overlapping interests. These systems — banking institutions, military institutions and their vendor companies, governments, unions, special interest groups, manufacturers, retailers, real estate developers, entertainment companies, media conglomerates and so on — all of these systems are all struggling to survive in Darwinian fashion. They are all made up of managers trying to advance their careers or protect their professional fiefdoms or maybe just keep their employees from getting fired. They are made up of normal people looking out for themselves. Big and small businesses trying to grow. Managers of departments trying to justify their budgets. People with various interests asserting them. Boring stuff. Bureaucracy.

These are basic human survival strategies that have been playing out in some form or another for all of recorded history. International trade isn't new. Businessmen didn't just start wanting to make more money. Governments didn't just start being corrupt, and they didn't just now start seeking assistance from businessmen who had lots of money. There has never in the history of the world been such a thing as an "objective" media. And self-serving bureaucrats have been around for thousands of years.

But until recently, nations remained nations. They were nations of place, language, religion and race. People living in different nations developed and maintained distinctly different cultures. People believed different things and incompatible religious groups fought turf wars. The sexes had different social roles. People had ethic roots that they were willing to fight for. They weren't so quick to trade away their ethnic identities and the identities of their ancestors to disappear into "the future"... into the vagueness of "progress."

Why did the West, a collection of nations with different languages and histories, a collection of kingdoms and proper Empires, become a collection of businesses and institutions aligned against identity? How did the cultural hegemony imposed by the West on others become the culture of cultural erasure?

THE MOTHER OF EXILES

Moral universalism has roots in Classical philosophy and has been perpetuated by religions that claim to be the one true religion for all man and womankind. But even these one-size-fits-all creeds have splintered, often violently, into sects. Their adherents have frequently put aside their love for all mankind to fight for race or nation.

Universal, convert-or-kill faiths like Christianity or Islam have harmonized well with expansive cultures and expanding Empires, and laid much of the moral and philosophical groundwork for the all-inclusive, culture-erasing universalism that is epidemic in the West and spreading virulently across the globe.

But religions have rules. Religions have ideals. Religions that claim to be the best way, the true way, and the only right way for all men and women all around the world must punish, shun or exclude those who behave the wrong way. Every right way is defined against its opposite. Piety and right-living are contrasted against heresy and sin. Even this has become inconvenient.

The universalism of today, the universalism that can only condemn those who condemn and separate those who separate is the product of global commerce. The one true god of the universalist is Mammon, and he embraces anyone with cash who doesn't scare away other customers. This is why we are told to accept the unacceptable, to condemn religions that condemn, to share cultures with everyone as if they belong to no one, to deny all racial affinity, to pretend that men and women are interchangeable. Because exclusion is bad for business.

If you run the only gas station in town, you can alienate whoever you want, but if you have to compete for business with a gas station across the street who welcomes everyone, the other guy is probably going to do better, especially in a mixed community. Your ability to expand and attract new business will be limited by the number of people you are willing to serve. Exclusion is limitation.

The small or single businessman is relatively insignificant in the age of the publicly traded corporation with international reach. The publicly traded corporation is fundamentally and by the very charter of its existence amoral. The only true purpose of a publicly traded company is to deliver a return on the investment of its shareholders, and shares may be purchased by anyone with money. The publicly traded company accepts investments from anyone, and in order to continue to expand and increase its profits and deliver a return on those investments, it must find a way to peddle its wares to everyone.

Whether a company sells software or soft porn or soft drinks, the tendency of policy must always be toward expansion and inclusion. If one included group takes offense that another group is included, the group that takes offense can be made to seem intolerant, bigoted, backwards and hateful. The commercial spirit rises above all of that. The global corporation transcends race, sex, nation and religion. Godlike, it loves all the little children of the world, hears all of their prayers, answers them with products — and accepts payment in every currency.

When the universalism of this age is understood as grease on the gears of global commerce, when contemporary universalism is understood as a commercial ethos that has superseded all religious, tribal, cultural and rational moral systems, the ecstatic zealotry of today's moral crusaders is easily explained and understood.

The human tendency toward witch-hunting, exposing sin and silencing heretics has been turned by the sniping gossips and crowd-shamers of this age against any obstacle to the kind of complete human interchangeability that makes the most sense on the spreadsheets of bankers. The sins of the universalist age are words or actions that separate, discriminate, differentiate or evaluate people. The sinners condemned are those who condemn, the only people who can be publicly discriminated against are those who discriminate.

No non-violent behavior can be judged or criticized except the behavior of those who judge or criticize anything but the most banal and inconsequential consumer choices — like what someone wore or what car they bought. People still naturally giggle and gossip, as they have for thousands of years, about social awkwardness and who-fucked-who, but passionate moral condemnation and public shaming are now reserved for racists, sexists, religious "extremists" and all of the phobes: homophobes, xenophobes, transphobes, Islamophobes and and anyone else who limits or excludes or defines by separating or distinguishing.

This tactic of associating all non-universalist moralities with fear is itself a shrewd subversion of male honor. By equating any discriminatory position with cowardice, lonely male consumers without the sense of identity and belonging that comes from a strong group of bonded male peers can be easily manipulated by their natural desire to avoid association with groups of men who are socially recognized as cowards.

In this universalist age, all violence except state violence is condemned, and state violence is deployed under the banner of reducing "extremism," or "separatism," or any threat to domestic peace and international unity. There are no true enemies, only potential allies — hearts and minds yet to be won, "peaceful people" being deprived of their natural right to fast food, wall-to-wall carpet and high definition pornography. There are no more statues of heroes because no true villains can be acknowledged. There is no Beowulf because there are no monsters or dragons — only outsiders who are disenfranchised and misunderstood. Monuments can only be raised to mythic martyred unifiers like Jesus Christ or Martin Luther King or Abraham Lincoln.

This moral universalism that serves commerce, this idea that anyone is as good as his pile of gold, must have been present to some extent in any center of trade at any point in history. It follows logically when there is opportunity to trade with a wide range of people, and when competition for business has eclipsed all other loyalties, moralities and concerns, as it has today. The soft and "open-minded" civilities of urban merchants have long been at odds with male tribalism and honor cultures.

Classical ideas and religions-for-all may have facilitated universalist moralities, but tribalism and the moral absolutes of religions have checked the expansion of mercantile universalism. However, at least two other factors specific to the 20th and early 21st Centuries have allowed the universalism that attends commerce to overpower all other allegiances, ideologies and even basic acknowledgements of human nature.

First, there has been an explosion of technology that has connected geographically distant groups of people in ways that were formerly impossible. Affordable international travel, followed by television and the media, have connected people who previously never would have met. Cultures develop in some sort of isolation, and isolation today must increasingly be a deliberate choice. The default mode is to constantly hear news and information about strangers hundreds or thousands of miles away, creating a false sense of proximity and personal connection to everyone, everywhere. Western people often do business with or speak to people in different states, nations or continents more often than they interact with their own neighbors. Cultural boundaries are crossed, differences are minimized. People who will never meet use the same software, buy the same clothes, play the same games, use the same tools, watch the same shows, listen to the same music. Global trade creates universal cultural experiences shared by virtually everyone. People everywhere share cultural experiences well beyond the basic experience of being humans on Earth.

Science and medicine have also revealed how similar all humans are. Most humans share the same basic needs, suffer from the same physical ailments, struggle with similar psychological problems, and can be manipulated predictably in the same ways. Small differences between the aptitudes and attitudes of different groups of people who evolved in different environments are either denied, made to seem insignificant, or bred out through mixed marriages.

Throughout history one of the most consistent strategies employed to unify patrimonial groups into tribes, kingdoms and nations has been the discovery or manufacture of a mythical common ancestor. Today, modern genetic and evolutionary studies are frequently employed in the service of global unity to show that all humans have common ancestors, even if their ancestral groups separated millions of years ago and the relevance of common ancestry is questionable. Science has merely replaced myth and religion in supplying the most expedient unifying narrative.

Many believe that they have "evolved beyond" their tribal instincts, or that they have critically examined racial, sexual and cultural differences and made a conscious decision, based on the information available to them, to deal with others "objectively" or overcompensate to correct their own perceived prejudices, which are always assumed to be incorrect or unfair or morally wrong. The idea that you are one of millions of people around the world who independently reasoned his or her way beyond racism, sexism and cultural bias is an obnoxiously vain fantasy. Being anti-racist and anti-sexist and accepting of cultural differences is not a product of your own independent thought, it is the prevailing spirit of this commercial age, facilitated by global informational infrastructures and taught by nearly every educational institution in the civilized world. Being anti-racist or anti-sexist or culturally tolerant today is like being Catholic during the Middle Ages or the Renaissance. It's a culturally enforced social norm, and like the old Catholics, today's average "objective critical thinker" will gleefully support any witch hunt or Inquisition aimed at the enemies of the Universalist faith. The same madness of crowds continues in a different form.

The second unusual factor that facilitates commercial universalism in the present age is the unprecedented political and cultural influence of women, which has transformed their talents for nurturing and peacemaking into a pathological form of universal altruism.

It has always been the job of men to separate "us" from "them," and to police and protect the boundaries of the band, tribe, kingdom or nation. The function of women has always been to unify the tribe from within, to nurture positive relationships, to make everyone feel wanted and included, and to care for and empathize with the young, the old, the sick and the wounded.

Women, especially high status women, have always exerted political influence through their men. For instance, throughout the Icelandic sagas and other Germanic literature, one learns again and again that if you anger the queen, she will use her influence over the king and his men to make you pay for it. However, after women were given a formal and equal vote in democratic societies, their natural tendencies to nurture, comfort, and include quickly corroded the cultural structures of those societies both internally and externally.

Internally, in terms of domestic policy and everyday life, natural and functional hierarchies have been progressively undermined or eliminated. Competitiveness has been de-emphasized to the point where "everyone's a winner," so that no one suffers for being a loser. High physical standards are relaxed to include the unworthy and unqualified, even in demanding physical professions like law enforcement, firefighting and the military. Wealth is extorted from the successful and redistributed to anyone who says they need it, reducing both motivation to succeed and the penalties of failure. Female sympathy for victims of disease or circumstance has elevated victimhood to heroic levels, actually making victimhood so desirable that even the most spoiled of white women degrade themselves by publicizing maudlin, mundane and often made-up tales of private trauma or personal struggle. The sweet sympathy of a mother for a child whose feelings have been hurt are extended almost indiscriminately across society, so that nearly every hurt or perceived hurt is treated with legitimate concern with no responsibility placed on the individual — there can be no "blaming the victim." Moves must be made to nurture and protect every potential victim from injury, even if that is impossible. Like the goddess Frigg asking fire, water, iron, beasts and birds to take an oath to protect her son, the nature of woman, unchecked by men, is to child-safe the world and try to save us all from anything that could do us harm...*or bring us glory.*

And, whereas female empathy helps intratribally and within families to help parties see both sides of a disagreement and reconcile their differences, when female empathy is applied intertribally, the effect is never-ending inclusiveness. The points of view of outsiders and enemies are considered and they are invited in without regard to how it might alter or corrupt the tribe. Both social and national borders are viewed as overly formal, and men are scolded for voicing practical or tactical concerns about the indiscriminate inclusion of immigrants, refugees and individuals who express values that conflict with the existing values of the tribe. Everyone must be sympathized with, invited, and accepted. Eventually, no one can be banished but the banishers.

Women have always excelled at teaching and enforcing everyday etiquette. Within a given tribe, this has always been a necessary and important role that promotes internal unity and harmony. It was probably a woman who first taught you basic manners — when to say "please" and "thank you" and what kinds of things you shouldn't say to other people if you wanted to get along in life.

Today, in the classroom, in the workplace, in the government and in the media, women are among the foremost proponents of all forms of political and social correctness. If there is someone with a megaphone shouting "racist" or "sexist" or "hateful" it is probably a woman or an effeminate man. Women are behaving as they have always behaved and are playing similar roles, but instead of serving the tribe, they have become the useful idiots of global financial interests who use their newfound political influence to mommy us all, weaken us by protecting us from risk, and reconcile away any meaningful tribal identities that could interrupt the expansion of global commerce.

Emma Lazarus' poem, "The New Colossus," which is found at the base of The Statue of Liberty, serves as an early sketch of what Americanism reinterpreted by women would feel like.

"The New Colossus"

Not like the brazen giant of Greek fame,
With conquering limbs astride from land to land;
Here at our sea-washed, sunset gates shall stand
A mighty woman with a torch, whose flame
Is the imprisoned lightning, and her name
Mother of Exiles. From her beacon-hand
Glows world-wide welcome; her mild eyes command
The air-bridged harbor that twin cities frame.
"Keep, ancient lands, your storied pomp!" cries she
With silent lips. "Give me your tired, your poor,
Your huddled masses yearning to breathe free,
The wretched refuse of your teeming shore.
Send these, the homeless, tempest-tossed to me,
I lift my lamp beside the golden door!"

— Emma Lazarus, 1883

The pathological altruism of the matriarchal thinker who wants to take in and nurture everyone from everywhere has come into harmony with the commercial perspective that "everyone's money is good."

The Mother of Exiles is wedded to Mammon. Together they stand against ancient identities and history as they welcome the refuse of the world into the global marketplace.

Come all ye faithless, and spend!

FREEDOM

The Mother of Exiles will welcome you into Mammon's Empire of Nothing.

She will embrace you and accept you, whoever you are. She will tell you that you are special. She will comfort and affirm you. She will assure you that your weaknesses are strengths. She wants to hear your story, no matter how dull or sad, and agrees that you've been victimized and treated unfairly. She values "equality" above all things, and if you are handicapped in spirit or aptitude, she will handicap the capable to make life feel more "fair." Held tight to her bosom, you will never feel unsafe or uncomfortable for long, because if you do, she'll motion to Father Mammon's Imperial Guard to intimidate or whisk away the bad men.

The Mother of Exiles announces herself as a beacon of Freedom.

She doesn't mind what you wear or what band posters you hang on your wall. You can have sex with whoever you want in your room, no questions asked. She'll bake you pot brownies and give you all of the sugary beverages you want while you play games with your friends. She'll always be there to save you from yourself with barriers and guidelines designed to protect you from physical harm. Just keep breathing and putting tokens in the machine.

The Mother of Exiles offers the warm freedom of the womb.

The People of the Empire have been convinced that they are free. They are free to do anything but leave the Mother's womb, to distinguish and separate themselves from The Empire — to be born.

The People of the Empire have been convinced that freedom is a synonym for permission. They believe they are free because they've won the permission to smoke marijuana in their own homes, marry a person of the same sex, or to change their sex altogether if they don't like being a male or a female. They believe that they are free because they are permitted to purchase permits to buy handguns or build houses. The People of the Empire believe they are free because they are allowed to vote and officially register their opinions. They are even permitted to protest — peacefully.

When men fight for freedom, they aren't fighting for permission.

When men fight for freedom, they are fighting for independence and self-determination. Except in the case of slave revolts, they are fighting for collective determination. When free men fight together for freedom, they are fighting for separation to establish a new collective identity. They are fighting to distinguish a new "us" from an old "us" which has become a tyrannical "them." They are drawing a new perimeter and establishing a new order.

Within the boundaries of the Empire, secession movements are rarely allowed to succeed. In America, the Southern states agreed through open debate and democratic process to legally separate themselves from the United States of America to protect their own interests and their own culture. The United States government refused to allow secession, and preferred to have 620,000 men die in order to retain access to Southern wealth and resources. One wonders how "free" Americans have really ever been since.

If you're not allowed to leave peacefully, you're not "free."

The Empire of Nothing was in its infancy then, and it was still considered normal for people to maintain separate national, ethnic, religious, racial and sexual identities. Even Lincoln, storied savior of unifiers, wanted to send emancipated black slaves away to a colony of their own.

But time has passed and the Empire has expanded, and collective separation of any kind will no longer be entertained. The aim of the Empire of Nothing is social atomization — a splitting of groups into smaller groups, then families, then finally the individual. The individual is convinced that his individuality is a total identity, and that he is better and stronger for standing alone. However, a man alone is actually quite easy to manage, to coerce, to destroy. The individual is rarely a meaningful threat to the ethos of the Empire without some kind of support network. A man or a woman or a "genderless person" alone is merely a sum of aptitudes, skills, wants and preferences. He, she, or it is conveniently manageable and utterly dependent on the Empire, floating in the void of billions as a set of numbers on millions of spreadsheets.

This is *their* future.

Weakness and solitude. Emptiness feeding consumption and a feeling of powerlessness that seeks the illusion of agency. Total unity and total interchangeability.

For the average man, this means progressive emasculation as well as the elimination and stigmatization of male-only groups of any kind. It means a monoculture of everything for everyone. It means the abandonment of sincere religion, and eventually of all racial, ethnic and sexual identity. The model citizen of The Empire of Nothing is a citizen of the Empire — of the World — first and foremost. All other residual, subcultural and consumer identities must remain subordinate to the identity of World Citizen and Consumer.

Any identity that supersedes the identity of World Citizen is a revolt against the Empire and a motion toward freedom — toward traumatic separation from the Mother of Exiles and birth into the world.

One does not simply go to war with an Empire at the peak of its power — especially not an Empire that is capable of observing almost everything you do in real time. This isn't the American Revolution. There is no ocean in the way, and you won't be fighting men in red coats with muskets. The Empire has "Predator" and "Reaper" drones at its disposal. The Empire has all the money in the world. To plan an armed revolt from within the borders of The Empire of Nothing would guarantee law enforcement action and annihilation.

The weakness of The Empire of Nothing is that it probably isn't run by Reptilians. Like every other Empire in history, it is run by people, and it requires the obedience and cooperation of its subjects to function and expand. And like all Empires, it relies on maintaining a superordinate culture to assimilate and enlist the conquered. The conquering narrative of the Empire of Nothing is a narrative of total unity. In exchange for accepting the narrative, the Empire offers a comforting, multicultural hospice as you pass into the void.

Universalist ideologies, whether Christianity or Islam or communism or commercial multiculturalism, all have the ultimate goal of world unity and submission. No matter what it takes to get there, the end is the same. Billions of peaceful, interchangeable people on their knees. Total submission. Total nothingness. One identity to end all identity. One story to end all stories.

The unifying narrative of the Empire may simply be the latest evolution of the universal death cult.

The only way to gain freedom from the Empire is to undermine that narrative with counter-narratives. To create alternative stories and identities. The meat grinder of universal togetherness can only be opposed by tribal separateness. Not mere subcultures, but tribes of people with exclusive identities who resist assimilation and exist as independently as possible. Tribes of people who are truly connected, and who are more loyal to each other than they are to the Empire. Tribes of people who are willing to build social barriers and nurture cultures and values that are distinctly separate from the culture and values of the Empire.

The strength of this approach is that humans naturally want to belong to a group. They are hungry for identity, because identity is meaning, identity is order — identity is everything. The Empire sells superficial identities that are fleeting, synthetic, empty and unsatisfying. In a world of single, spoiled boys who have been able to walk away from any commitment or association — lifetime brotherhood is a radical idea. Collective honor is a radical idea. Working to help people you know and care about instead of strangers is a radical idea.

The point is not to be oppositional for the sake of being oppositional. These ideas are radical in that they are at odds with the social agenda of The Empire, but they are appealing because they are also ancient, profound and fundamentally human. The word radical itself comes from the Latin word for root. Tribalism is the root of human culture.

If you want to be free in the way your ancestors would have understood freedom — if you want more than permission and comfort and obligatory affirmation — then plant a new root or tend an old one. Start a tribe or join one. Make bold mistakes. Contribute to the growth of a social organism strong enough to survive and thrive in the arid nothingness of modernity. Show people the real thing that they've been looking for, the thing that they've tried to buy.

It may not be about you or your survival. You may not live to see it reach its final height or perfect form. In fact, if you do it right, you probably won't.

There's an old Greek proverb that says, "society grows great when old men plant trees whose shade they know they shall never sit in."

If you don't like what's happening around you, what's happening to culture, what's happening to men and women, what people are becoming — get out there and start digging. Plant the seed of something new. Of something better. Plant the seed of something you really want — not just whatever you think you can have. Show others that there's a different way to live.

Spend the rest of your life tending a root that may one day grow into a tree of liberty.

"...Moses knew that he couldn't create a society of free men from a generation born as slaves. Moses kept his people wandering until the previous generation had died..."

— Chuck Palahniuk, *Fight Club 2 : Issue #3*

BECOMING A BARBARIAN

The rest of this book is about changing your mind.

It's about becoming the kind of man who could become a member of a tribe and thrive, spiritually, outside of The Empire of Nothing. It's a rough sketch of some of the psychological airlocks you'll have to move through to stop thinking like one of the Empire's interchangeable slaves to thinking like a man with a complete identity and a sense of belonging to a people.

Men everywhere yearn for the collapse of this current mode of civilization that, as an inevitable consequence of its design, must devalue and emasculate them. Apocalyptic fantasies are a particularly male preoccupation. More and more men are focusing on survivalism and preparedness to give themselves a sense of purpose in a world that doesn't need or want them to be strong, courageous or prepared for anything.

However, many seem determined to survive some ordeal only to rebuild the same civilization, incorporating the same egalitarian, universalist, trade-oriented values that wil inevitably lead to the same end. If you rebuild the Mother of Exiles and light a lamp for all of the huddled masses and wretched refuse of the world without regard for race, religion or tradition, you will end up with the same money-driven matriarchal mess of self-loving bonobos you currently see before you. The founding values of America's Founding Fathers — or their omission of values — are the foundation of the problem. If you are not explicit about separating "us" from "them," however that boundary is defined, you will end up with an Empire of Nothing and everything at the same time. Pluralism may be born out of necessity or base opportunism, but it is ultimately neurotic.

Adopting a tribal mindset means abandoning pluralism for good. It means choosing a few out of the many. To Empire-trained ears, the tribal man may come off as cultish and cruel. Objectivity is rarely more than a pose, but the tribal man may seem especially and proudly biased, dismissive, unreasonable and unscientific to any outsider. Choosing to care completely for a few and refusing to care at all for the many will seem callous, but caring for a few sincerely means truly knowing and caring about people instead of being manipulated into emoting theatrically about strangers. The tribal man will seem immoral, but members of his tribe will demand far more of him morally than bureaucrats, fair weather friends and business associates. The tribal man will be seen as a parasite, because he takes from the Empire for his people and gives nothing to the Empire in return. Tribal interests run counter to the universalistic ethos of this commercial age, so men who are tribal may be regarded as criminals by those charged with protecting commercial interests. The tribal man will have to re-think what it means to him to be regarded as an outlaw or a parasite or a monster to the people of the Empire. He will have to reconsider whose denouncements truly matter.

The rest of this book will challenge you to explore these changes of the mind.

The collapse may be imminent and its doomsayers may be vindicated, but waiting for the world to start is not the same as starting it. People can begin to think tribally, act tribally, and build tribal networks and cultures now, as both a revolt against the commercial Empire and a preparation for possible collapse. Insular tribal networks such as those maintained by immigrant communities and staunch religious groups offer workable models of communal interdependence that would make their members more resilient in an emergency than "independent" moderns who would trust state and corporate agencies to "care" for them. And perhaps, in creating alternatives to the commercial Empire, these rebels can undermine its messaging and hasten its decline.

The word barbarian comes to us from the Greeks, who regarded non-Greeks — those who babbled in their own foreign tongues or who spoke Greek badly — with civilized contempt. It doesn't describe a particular people. A barbarian is an outsider, someone with a separate culture who is not part of the state or polis. The word barbarian is evidence of the Greeks thinking tribally. They weren't afraid to separate "us" (meaning: "us Greeks") from "them" (meaning: "Who cares? They aren't even Greek!").

In the past, barbarians were outsiders in both a cultural sense and a physical sense. They were from somewhere else. The lived beyond the reach of the Empire's borders and raided its edges and frontiers. This is no longer possible, because the Empire is everywhere.

Flag-wavers often say, "If you don't like my country, then leave." But there is nowhere to go. There is no escape. There are no more New Worlds, no readily habitable and fertile uncharted lands to discover. The reach of commercialism and its universalist monoculture is always expanding, even into unstable and untamed zones like Africa or Afghanistan, and it will keep expanding until there is a McDonalds in every Mosque and the world's most volatile religion is moderated into another meaningless consumer identity. You could spend all of your resources and the best years of your life trying to fuck off to some rugged oasis, only to find a few years later that Globocorp will be bulldozing your eden to make room for chain stores and condominiums.

Men who were born within the pegged together particle board and plastic Empire are not and cannot become blissfully ignorant bug and banana eaters. Almost all men are products of the Empire, born in concrete hospitals and brought up gobbling processed sugar snacks while kept busy with cartoons. All they have is a dream of a different life and a sense that everything worth having is being systematically snuffed out to make way for more weakness and empty greed and semi-solitary sloth. Men born into the Empire cannot go back and be born barbarians or run away to some magical place to become barbarians. The only way to become barbarians today is to create that magical place inside the Empire, hollow out little pockets inside of it and become outsiders who undermine the Empire within its borders.

Becoming an outsider within is similar to what Ernst Junger called "the forest passage." When one cannot escape modernity, one must secede spiritually and nurture a world within a world. Junger believed that each of us carries some unquantifiable grain of primordial existence, something alive that allows us to see a forest of life and meaning even in the desert of the mechanized modern world. He imagined his forest rebels as lone wolves, but as the necessary revolt against modern universalism is tribalism, packs of wolves are required. Men must become packs of werewolves — civilized men who transform themselves into something wild and alien to the Empire, carrying the forest with us even in when surrounded by metal and glass, making unbreakable bonds amidst millions of fair-weather "friends" and superficially concerned strangers.

This transformation from civilized man into wolf, from bureaucratic thinker to barbarian, necessitates a spiritual revolution — a profound change in thinking and approach to both big issues and everyday challenges. The littlest thing, like paying attention to the way you use the word "we," has broad philosophical implications.

WHO IS "WE?"

"We The People..."

"We, as a society..."

"We are the world..."

It is something of a paradox that Westerners and particularly Americans, being among the most fiercely individualistic people in the world, have also developed a habit of speaking in broad, collectivist terms. It's a convention of modern speech and writing to address everyone democratically, as if "we" are all are going to come to some sort of agreement.

People are always rattling on about what "we" should do, whether they are talking about "their" country or "their" race or all of humanity or some other abstract group of humans who don't give a damn what they think about anything.

Who is "We?" Who can you legitimately speak for? Who cares what you say?

If you don't know, you're just running your mouth. You're just some guy yelling at the TV during a football game. Your "we" can't hear you and if they could, they wouldn't care anyway.

Even men who know better in theory, who know that their votes are all but meaningless and who know in their hearts and minds that the government of the territory in which they reside operates entirely without their consent...even many of these guys still spout off about what "we" should do or who "we" should bomb at the slightest national crisis or emergency.

This habitual invocation of the multitude in speech, writing and thought has become a psychological fetter of the Empire of Nothing. A man who speaks for the ambiguously collective "we" remains confined within the Empire's spiritual territory.

The finite scope of the American "we" is a remnant of tribal instinct, but as the policies of most modern Western governments are more oriented toward globalism than nationalism, this old patriotic spirit is merely exploited to serve universalist causes. So long as these universalist policies continue, any use of the word "we" referring to a Western state logically serves neither a particular people nor culture, but ultimately the much broader sprawl of humanity, in addition to the economic elites and managerial classes who benefit most conspicuously from globalist orientations. The patriotic "we the people" has become little more than a sentimental attachment to territory, a love of local history, an idolatry of antiques and a fondness for a cherry-picked selection of ideas which have long since been discarded in practice by those who preside over the institutions wrapped in their regalia. This flag-waving "we" is just another sports team with tradable and interchangeable players, engaged in friendly competition within the same expanding league. Your job is to cheer for the team associated with your geographic region. As long as you keep wearing your team colors and keep giving directions to the players on the field as if they could hear you — as if they would care — you will always be a citizen of the Empire.

Evaluating and altering the way you use the word "we" in speech, thought and writing is the simplest, yet also one of the most profound changes you can make in your everyday life to secede psychologically from the global collective and become a barbarian.

As a corrective exercise, stop yourself every time you are about to use the word "we."

Work through the following thought process:

» **Describe or identify exactly which people you are referring to.**

» **Also, examine who you are you not referring to.**

» **Determine approximately how many people are in that group.**

» **Evaluate the your influence within that group — what is the likelihood that the people in this group will care about what you have to say, think or write?**

» **Do the other people in this group know that they are in a group with you?**

» **Would the other people in this group acknowledge you as a representative member?**

» **What would other members of this group do for you if you needed help?**

» **What would you do for them, if they needed help?**

» **Do the majority of the people in this group share your values? Are you sure?**

As you consciously track and evaluate your own use of the word "we," you will probably also become more aware of how often and how casually others use words like "we" or "us" to associate themselves with wide ranges of people. Most people "rep" the word "we" many times a day. In some small way, with each repetition they are affirming their perceived membership in a group as part of their identity.

Of course, it is occasionally practical to speak in broad terms about the tendencies or patterns of behavior common among large groups of people with whom you share some background or experience, just as it is often practical to identify patterns of behavior in other groups.

I live in a territory ruled by the American government. I am a white male. I am a Westerner. While I try to avoid it, I'm sure I've recently — perhaps even somewhere in this book — included myself as an American or a white man or a Westerner by using the word "we." It's a convenient shorthand.

However, I have been careful about my use of collective speech, working through roughly the same thought process described above, for several years now. When I mean the American government, I say "the American government." I do this because I've come to the conclusion that the American government is a "them," not a "we." As the old saying goes: "say what you mean and mean what you say."

So many people who live in America complain about the way "most Americans" behave, but still consider Americans "us" and use the word "we." Why? Why are you stuck with these people? Because you live in the same area? Do you feel obligated to show solidarity with every baby born and every immigrant who crosses the border? Is there no limit to the number of humans to whom you will feel obligated in this way, so long as they reside within a set of geographical boundaries? Who are you allowing to make that determination for you? Do you honestly believe that the people making those decisions care about your prosperity and happiness? If so, based on what evidence or history of action?

The national "we," is only one example. People speak in collective terms about species, race, sex, sexuality — even as fans of a particular band or genre of music or television show. Religion, particularly, is a great "uniter" that ultimately ends up dividing people. Christianity is supposed to be for everyone in theory, but in accordance with human nature, Christians have historically drawn unforgiving lines between "us" and "them" amongst themselves. A history of sectarian violence among white Christian Europeans likely contributed to the "big-tent" deism and pluralism of many of America's Founding Fathers. Today, a conversation about Christianity with a Christian will often start out in broad, inclusive statements about what "we Christians believe," and progress to exclude, "those Christians" or "those people who aren't even really Christians."

These distinctions are a perfectly natural consequence of carefully determining what you actually believe, and who you honestly feel connected to. As you define your groups with greater precision, they will almost always become smaller. However, by abandoning the comfort of platitudes and carefully assessing your legitimate connections and true "human resources," you are increasing the accuracy of your observations and improving your sense of your own orientation in the world. 'We' is who is left when shit gets real. Knowing the difference between your "we" and your "they" will inevitably influence the way you make decisions about how to act. Your OODA loop becomes more realistic, and therefore more effective. Identifying who and what really matters in your world is also grounding and clarifying. It will give you a clearer sense of direction.

A sober assessment of your reciprocal human relationships may also be depressing. Many modern men can count on one hand the number of other men who they could actually depend on in an emergency — or even ask to borrow $100. Some men have no one at all, and are entirely dependent on the benevolence of the government, corporations and other big collections of strangers.

This is the way of the Empire.

To be a barbarian today is to draw your own perimeter and build social networks and reciprocal relationships that are not dictated or controlled by the Empire. It means drawing in the boundaries of your "we" so that you know exactly who your people are, who you can depend on, who cares about what happens to you, who you are obligated to, and where your loyalties lie. It's easy to say that you "belong" to big, abstract groups of strangers who demand nothing of you. Becoming a barbarian — becoming the kind of man who can belong to a tribe — requires a level of commitment that makes "good, modern, civilized men" uncomfortable.

BELONGING IS BECOMING

Hail the rugged individualist!

You are both a man and an island, a lonely lighthouse standing boldly and brightly shining your skeptic's light of objective truth over the murky sea of uncertainty and confusion.

You wouldn't join any club that would have you as a member — which is just your smug, jokey way of saying you think groups are for suckers and you are far too smart to lose yourself in the snake-handling, sig-heiling, hymn-singing madness of crowds.

Western men are in love with the Hobbesian fallacy that the natural state and truest form of man is a man alone, fiercely independent, and at war with the world. They are in love with the idea of being ronin armed with reason, masterless men doing battle against falsehood, true only to their own personal sense of honor and somehow too pure to be corrupted by involvement with "group-thinkers."

The Hollywood ideal is the damaged do-gooder, a tumbleweed of restless violence and God's Own Truth blowing from storyline to storyline, refusing or botching all franchise-endangering attachments. The popularity of the do-right drifter endures because he both captures and romanticizes the isolation of a man lost in the scale of modern social organization. In this narcissistic fantasy, modern men can attribute a moral nobility to what is, for all but a few, complete statistical irrelevance and state-sponsored separation from groups of men unsupervised by women or bureaucratic functionaries.

The knight-errant with no round table suits the universalist Zeitgeist perfectly. Every man owes his allegiance to everyone and no one at the same time, and he is pitted only against his own perception of "evil" in the service of that which is good for all man and woman-kind. He wanders through crowds alone, and alone, he can do very little harm to any established interests. He feels all-powerful, the captain of his own soul, but except in the rarest of cases he is all but inconsequential.

We are constantly reassured that "one person can really make a difference" precisely because the opposite is true. Maybe one person with a billion dollars, but not just one person. The lone wolf can snarl and snap at the heels of the governments and corporations, but he is always dismissed by the powers that be as a friendless nut-job — a true individualist! The democratic doctrines of individual power and universal responsibility are stultifying, pacifying pipe dreams for plebeian wage slaves who work with strangers and commute home to the lonely blue light of their opinionating stations to submit their oh-so-important views and votes.

The best men are not loners, they are leaders. The best men, the greatest exemplars of virility, are not the spoiled, decadent inheritors of crowns and laurels — they are the men who earn the respect, trust and admiration of other men in their own lifetimes. Men who do not lead are not empowered by always going it alone. They become the best, most powerful versions of themselves by working in concert with other men, bringing everything they have and using it to accomplish more than they could accomplish by themselves.

The unaffiliated individualist, the free-thinking seeker of truth and justice, wary of bias, stereotyping, prejudice and privilege... is not free at all. He is a self-master in his own mind, but he is more dependent on people who care about him less. He is dependent on theoretically impartial institutions, bureaucratic infrastructures and profit-seeking corporations for all of his basic needs, and his ability to influence those institutions and corporations is negligible. He cannot approach them as a man who has earned the respect of his peers. No, he can only grovel at their complaint desks, submitting grievances and filing lawsuits. As these institutions expand and become ever more inclusive, his influence becomes even less powerful. In a sea of billions, a man alone is plankton.

He is lost and adrift, but drifts alone because his greatest fear is losing himself.

Psychoanalysts sometimes use an iceberg as a model for the psyche. Our conscious selves are the tip of the iceberg that sticks out of the water. This protruding portion of the iceberg is made up of of our ego, what we think of as our rational mind and free will, along with a greater or lesser part of our superego, which includes our cultural training, morality and biases. Below the water lies the subconscious portion of the ego, most of the superego, and the weighty mass of the Id, made up of our primal drives. The Id is basic human nature.

The individualist has a religious devotion to his ego, and he strives to purify and protect it from the external influences that form the superego. The intellectual gunslinger, the lonely lighthouse is his self-schema — his romantic idea of himself. He will defend this idea of himself against the reality that the ego-worship of the individual and his "natural rights" has actually been the dominant cultural narrative in Western nations for two or three hundred years, and can be traced all the way back to Descartes' "I think, therefore I am." It is actually his superego, his training in cultural norms, as much as anything else, that tells him his ego is his greatest treasure. The individualist is terrified that his iceberg will sink, that he will become unconscious and lose his ego — himself — in the madness of the crowd, in the orgies of Id sanctioned by the superego.

The modern individualist — egoist, even — usually still talks about what everyone else talks about when they are talking about it, operates within a comfort zone of social norms and lives by himself in a way that is generally acceptable to what he calls, usually with some derision, "the herd." At his most individualistic, he is a troll, a heckler, a parasite. A troll can't be trusted, and should always be shunned and despised, even though it will only feed into his self-schema. At his least individualistic, the modern individualist becomes special just like everyone else. The familiar example is kids who are "trying to find themselves," who get involved in some "rebellious" subculture that has been carefully marketed to them, and spend their time and money hard signalling their belonging in some "individualistic" group. The adult individualist laughs at the hard-signalling teen from the comfort of his career khakis and settled life, but he is probably even less of an individual, and probably lonelier and less connected to anything. At least the youth subculture of the conforming "individualist" is a culture of connected people. Perhaps the older, more settled individualist's laugh is cynical and he has almost realized, where the waters of unconsciousness lap at his ego, that his individualism is and has always been a romantic lie.

The individualist protects himself from what he perceives as the unconsciousness of group-think, but by protecting himself from the dynamic judgment of the group, he also protects his ego from the truth and objectivity he claims to seek. He limits his development as a man, because man is not and has never been a solitary animal. The way of men has always been the way of the gang, and it is just as easy for him to delude himself about who and what he is alone as it is when running with a pack. Isn't it possible that a man knows less about himself when he protects himself like a rare zoological specimen, compared to the man who has observed himself in the wild, in the social formation that is most natural to his species? How mighty any caged ape seems, but his solitude prevents him from becoming what he truly is.

Do we really lose ourselves in a group, or do we become what we are? Perhaps, in a group, we develop along a particular route, which was one of many potential ways for us to be who we are, one reality out of many. Moreover, if we consciously choose a group and commit to it — which is, admittedly, not as normal for humans as patrimonialism but which has some precedence especially among the tribal Germanic peoples — are we not consciously directing our fate?

Surely, men do not become thoughtless zombies when they commit themselves to a group. Men in a tribe may participate in actions initiated by the group which they would not have initiated on their own, which they may or may not agree with completely, but as members of the tribe, like members of any functioning group of humans, they trade some free will for tangible and intangible benefits offered by the group. Every so-called individualist already does this, both by choice and in response to the coercive force of the state.

Men are always submitting to something or someone, whether in a gang or at work or to live in a nation of millions. It is the way of men to avoid being perceived as being overly submissive — we want to show strength and courage to each other and, tactically, to those who would threaten us. But every man either submits or compromises occasionally, or he dies very young. Submission is a normal and necessary feature of male psychology. Before acting, every man must consider the interests and the collective will of others in some way to be part of any group. Even pirate ship captains must consider the possibility of mutiny. Kings must address the strength of other nations and be wary of rebellions and civil wars and assassinations.

But because men respect the courage of the strong-willed, and weakness is dishonor, most men want to be seen as strong-willed. They will submit in some way or another, but they will want to believe and show the world that it is on their own terms. To compare male honor to female honor — they will want to show that they are not whores to be ravished by just anyone. They want to struggle and select before they relent, thereby maintaining their dignity. One might say that the difference between a free man and a slave is that the free man chooses his master.

Submission is a delicate subject for men. A man is supposed to be strong and courageous, so masculine submission seems like a paradox. But the relationship between masculinity and submission is one of those paradoxes made more paradoxical by words. Men reconcile the paradox easily enough in life, because they always have and it is in their nature to do so.

The barbarian has submitted to the will of his tribe. He has given up his freedom of association. Identity requires you to be someone, and not just anyone. Belonging to any group or society eliminates other options. The barbarian is tethered to the group and its worldview, while the individualist moves through the world easily and without much attachment.

But the tribal man is also free in ways a man afflicted with a universal morality can scarcely imagine. He moves through the world responsible to and for only a select group. He is not responsible for determining what is objectively true or universally right. He doesn't have to pretend to know the unknowable. He is concerned with what works, what doesn't, and what is best only for his people. By this measure, the barbarian is comparatively nimble, and sees with a practical clarity that is impossible for the man burdened and made tentative by a commitment to objective truth and universal right and wrong. To a tribal thinker with a properly functioning moral gear shift, your brother is your brother and others are others. That which is done in the service of the tribe is "right." The tribe is the superego, and the ego is free to put the Id to work for the brotherhood without conflict or hesitation.

The barbarian's ego is freed from universal moral responsibility, but it is not freed from all moral responsibility. He is not unconscious, as the individualist fears, but consciously working for his people. He has not lost his identity, but expanded it. He will be known to his people for his conduct, his actions and his talents. His worth will be checked and verified by his peers, instead of merely estimated by himself or a bunch of scolds and shopkeepers. In the words of Wolf Larsen, the value that life puts on itself is generally, "over-estimated since it is of necessity prejudiced in its own favour." The barbarian strives to become a legend in his tribe, not merely in his own mind.

For thinking men, the biggest psychological challenge to adopting a tribal mindset will be overcoming the fear of losing oneself in a group. Men have been taught that group-think is evil, and some level of groupthink is necessary for any group to function. But, even with no affiliations, every citizen of the Empire of Nothing lives and dies by a set of rules determined by others. Those others are almost always strangers. So much is already predetermined for the individuals of the Empire. Holding on to one's individualism is so often little more than a romantic mask for a fear of losing bourgeois respectability and an attachment to the material comforts afforded to the successfully conforming citizen. Men don't want to belong to any group because they don't want to be seen as weirdos or cult members and be socially ostracized. They don't want to be attached to anything that might keep them from getting work or making money. They don't want to attract the attention of law enforcement. The law of the Empire logically recognizes that any group of organized men who are more committed to each other than to others will undermine the mandate and the moral monopoly of the Empire. Men avoid joining groups in most cases because they are keeping their heads down — because they are already lost in the crowd of the Empire and they want to stay that way.

To become part of a tribe, you must be willing to let go of one version of yourself, one self-schema, and find another version of yourself within the context of the group. You must be willing to "lose yourself to find yourself." You must be willing to go to sleep in a world of rules determined by the Empire and wake up in a world of rules determined by the tribe. You must be willing to give up the inconsequential individualism of the citizen of the world and become an individual member of a tribe in which all of your assets, actions and ideas have an exponentially greater chance of being influential.

To leave the Empire behind and take on a tribal mind, you must choose to perceive that transformation not as an act of self-negation, but as a process of becoming and personal evolution. Belonging to a tribe is becoming.

The true self-loss is in giving yourself to billions — melting into the great expanse and becoming nothing more than another drop of water in the ocean.

"You never would have come here unless you believed you were going to save them. Evolution has yet to transcend that simple barrier. We can care deeply — selflessly — about those we know, but that empathy rarely extends beyond our line of sight."

— Dr. Mann, *Interstellar.* (2014)

NO TEARS FOR STRANGERS

It is true that all humans are genetically similar, that we suffer from many of the same diseases and ailments, that we share the same basic physical and psychological needs and wants. It is possible to empathize with the predicament of almost any human being, anywhere in the world. Thanks in part to advances in global communication and the weakening of ethnic and national spirits, humans all over the world now share similar cultural experiences. With the right camera angle, music and sensitive narration, we can put ourselves in almost anyone else's shoes.

But we don't — and can't — care about everyone on the planet. The idea that we can care about what is going on everywhere in the world is an illusion created by modern communication technology and the media. In truth, the human brain can't physically conceptualize billions or even millions of people as individuals with unique hopes and dreams and feelings. It is impossible to know and keep track of everything that is going on in a small city, state or nation. News networks pluck stories about people from all over the globe and deliver them to us in an easily digestible regurgitation.

While you were reading this, a child was molested. A man was beaten, or maybe raped by another man, or possibly murdered. Someone died of a drug overdose. Or cancer. Or a heart attack. An old woman collapsed, and she was a lot like your grandmother. There was a freak accident. A man suffered a life-changing injury at work. Someone was cheated by a salesperson or an insurance company or an employer.

Someone, somewhere suffered or died and you didn't care.

You didn't care, because no one told you to care.

If you cared or pretended to care about anything that happened to any stranger, you cared because the media selected a story for you to care about symbolically. Every week, executives and producers and editors and bloggers pick a handful of rapes, murders, atrocities, disasters, celebrity deaths, diseases, accidents, scandals and court cases for you to care about because those stories "popped" more than all of the rest of the human suffering that actually happened.

People care about those curated stories because no one has the time or the emotional energy or the brain processing power to care about every story. People care or ritualistically go through the motions of caring about those collected stories and doing so makes them feel connected to people all over the world.

They feel more connected, but they're not. Caring symbolically about strangers is not the same as caring about people who are close to you, and who you actually know. Caring symbolically about strangers is not improving human relationships. On the contrary, it often seems that those who make the biggest show of caring for the latest victimized group of faraway strangers tend to have strained or highly superficial relationships with those closest to them.

Most people don't think of "love" or "caring" or "friendship" as limited resources, but they are. "Caring" and "loving" are actions, and like all actions, they require time, effort and energy. Even when caring or loving are only thinking about caring or loving, thinking actively about one person means not thinking about someone or something else.

When you choose to care about a stranger on television, you are spending time and energy on a relationship that is not even superficial — it's non-existent. It's a complete fantasy. It's no different than caring about a character in a book or a film. You may believe that the person is real and the character is fake, but functionally, the emotional investment and the investment in time you are making in the distant stranger — the symbolic sufferer — is the same and completely one-sided in all but the rarest of circumstances. You are wasting your time, effort and energy on an imaginary relationship. Time spent investing in imaginary relationships is time not spent building real, reciprocal relationships. It's a retreat into a fantasy world that makes it possible for someone who spends a great deal of time caring about others to also be completely friendless, and have no one who cares about them...unless they somehow end up on the news.

From an economic standpoint, universal love — love spread among billions — is also worthless. It is offered to anyone in exchange for nothing. The love of a man who is willing to discriminate, to separate "us" from "them," has far greater value than the cheap sentiment of the man who says he loves all mankind. The love of a man who loves everyone and anyone is spread so thin it is weak and meaningless, but the love of man who discriminates is concentrated, powerful and profound. It gives him direction and purpose.

Adopting a tribal mindset puts an end to meaningless, one-sided, fantasy relationships with strangers and devoting all of your love, caring, loyalty and protection to a few out of the many. Becoming a barbarian means no tears for strangers, no matter how maudlin or real the presentation of their suffering.

That starving kid in Africa with flies on his eyes is still a stranger in some foreign shithole you'll never go to. He's not your responsibility, and the only reason you even know about him is because some group of people who would rather help exotic strangers than their own neighbors want you to give them money to continue their elaborate, self-gratifying social display of moral purity.

People are getting their heads sawed off by crazy-eyed jawas in the Middle East? Here's a pro-tip, fellas. Do not go to the Middle East. You are not welcome there. They still think tribally in that part of the world, and you are not part of their tribe. They don't play by your rules. You are not their people. You're an outsider, and they don't care if you live or die. You shouldn't care if they live or die either.

There's probably far more suffering and truly gory and insidious shit happening in China, but no one cares, and you never hear about it, because it's China. The Chinese don't even seem to care. Again, the only reason you know about "outrageous human rights violations" in the Middle East instead of somewhere else is because it is more important to people with a lot of money, power or both.

It is unlikely that you have power to significantly influence events in far-flung corners of the world or even down the block, so any emotional investment in political outcomes or the suffering of strangers overseas is a total waste of time, effort and energy that you could be investing in helping and building mutually beneficial relationships with people who you know, like or admire in your local area. Those investments are far more likely to yield a reciprocal return of love, caring, loyalty and even resources than investments in people you will never meet who live in places you will never go to.

Ask, "If I invested all of my time, energy and resources, up to and including my own life, to change this one thing, would it be reasonable for me to expect to alter the outcome of the situation?"

If the reasonable answer is "no," then surely your fickle, half-assed emoting about it is completely worthless.

The same is true even much closer to home. Even if you avoid television and social media and never listen to news on the radio, a simple trip to a grocery or convenience store will probably alert you to some new panic or riot or outrage or tragedy that everyone is supposed to care about one hundred or one thousand miles away. You will be inundated with stimuli designed, like the soundtrack to a movie, to invoke your sympathies or even your outrage. Taking the bait keeps you psychologically enslaved to the Empire of Nothing, to this interminable, desperate mass of interchangeable strangers vying for attention.

You can either choose to float invertebrate along the media's current and care about whoever the subjects of the Empire are caring about today, or choose to anchor your heart and mind to a select people and, like every comic book telepath, learn to tune out the cries of the multitude and focus your vitality on your people. Giving everything to your own people, to your own tribe, means leaving nothing for strangers. You must harden your heart or be at the mercy of the many. This is not hate. This is selective love, and practiced indifference. Your heart is like your eyes. Everything is a blur until you focus.

Every day you will hear about problems, and there will be millions more problems that you never hear about. Truly being there for your people, for a select group of people bound to you and you to them, will take more time and energy than you have. Everyone has problems. Chose whose problems matter to you. When pressed to care about strangers, the maxim of the modern barbarian loose in the Empire is:

"Not my people, not my problem."

THE MORAL GEAR SHIFT

To men who have been enslaved by the universalist creed that proclaims every man a brother, turning a blind eye to suffering will seem callous and immoral. Treating some people differently than others will seem unfair. Feeling obliged to help everyone, everywhere and to treat them all equally is the impossible and immobilizing burden of the universalist man. Woe to him who tries to move with the weight of the whole world's suffering on his back. To act, he must cheat and show preference, or do nothing at all — which is the only way he can truly treat everyone equally.

Universalist morality is the hypocritical creed of the Empire, so any alternative morality will necessarily be labeled "barbaric" by the mainstream. It may be "barbaric," to say that some people are more important to me than others, but it is far more honest than pretending I care about everyone equally. I don't, and neither do you. To care about everyone equally is inhuman, even sociopathic.

Those who go out of their way to show how much they care about strangers usually pick unpopular groups or exotic minorities to demonstrate their commitment to moral purity and compete for higher moral status within a universalist system. To bougie cosmopolitan status-seekers, it seems passé and clannish and even suspect for a white person to devote time and energy to helping other white people who have been wrongly convicted and who are rotting in prisons a few miles from their own homes. To eliminate the suspicion of preference, showing concern for Haitians or, better yet, some group no one has even heard of, sends a higher status signal to similarly privileged peers. Imagine the jaw-clenching, jealous smiles of the other ladies at some Seattle cocktail party when one woman reveals her commitment to help a group of recently discovered Khoikhoi refugees afflicted with Lyme disease and Tourette's.

The churchy, universal morality of the global mainstream appropriates moral principles that are extremely practical and unifying within a tribe or nation and perverts them by projecting these moral principles well beyond the horizon of human sight, perception and common interest.

Take, for instance, the idea of "fair play." It's non-religious and cross cultural. People are taught to "play fair," because the rules in a given game have been developed to mitigate the mortal risk of the game, and to encourage healthy competition while avoiding escalation into outright conflict. People are expected to be gracious winners and avoid being sore losers because games are just training for real conflict, and everyone involved goes home after the game and has to function as a productive member of the same larger society. In martial arts training, you don't actually try to cripple or kill your training partner during a simple drill, because you are training to kill or maim real enemies, not friends or training partners. So rules are observed.

"Playing fair" during real, life-or-death conflict is idiotic. There are no rules in actual war, only winners and losers. Modern Western "wars" are policing actions in which the major states of the world put leverage on groups of people who get out of line. They have the power to obliterate those people completely, but observe rules because they would rather bring them into the fold and look like "good guys." If you're serious about war, you burn villages full of women and children and put heads on stakes. Or you nuke a couple hundred thousand people in a few days. Likewise, if someone is attacking you and trying to kill you on the street, most places in America still recognize your personal right to use lethal force to defend yourself. There are no rules when you are actually in fear for your life. It's kill or be killed. There's no handshake or pat on the back after the game.

"Fairness" is conditional. There are different rules for different situations. There are different rules for friends and enemies, for outsiders and insiders.

The so-called Golden Rule of "Do Unto Others As You Would Have Them Do Unto You" is another example of a moral code that is practical and unifying within a tribe, but invites disaster when applied to those who are not bound to each other, to enemies, or to those whose own moral codes are completely unknown.

For instance, a man doing business in a small community lives and dies by his reputation, provided there is any competition for his services at al. It makes sense to be forthright, honest, dependable and agreeable, and even to "pay it forward" a bit by giving a little more than agreed to build goodwill within the community. If he is always doing shoddy work, or if he is rude, inconsiderate, or always cheating people and his word becomes worthless, people will stop offering him work or stop trading with him. Others in the same small community will have similar motivations, so treating others as he would like to be treated makes good sense.

In a city of hundreds of thousands or millions, one man could run around cheating people left and right, changing business names or addresses, and there would always be more suckers in line who hadn't heard about him from the last guy and wouldn't know to avoid him. A man from a small town doing business with the big city cheat would be a fool to assume a stranger outside of his small town's fast feedback loop would reciprocate his small town honesty and good faith. The Golden Rule works best in smaller, closed systems that share a common culture, while Caveat Emptor, Qui Bono, and "Do Unto Others As They Do Unto You" are far better mottoes for systems involving large, pluralistic groups of strangers.

When surrounded by strangers, while it is usually smart to be friendly, polite and easy to get along with to avoid unnecessary conflict and encourage similar behavior in others, adherence to The Golden Rule in matters of import with unknown individuals opens one up for easy exploitation. The Golden Rule is an excellent rule within a tribe and a foolish rule for dealing with the rest of the world.

Codes prohibiting or controlling violence provide the most dramatic example. It makes obvious strategic sense to punish people in a given tribe for maiming or murdering each other. Violence beyond the condoned and controlled violence of punishment or play spreads a sense of insecurity within the tribe, takes parents from their children, and by eliminating skilled individuals or able hands, may make the tribe weaker or less productive overall. The penalty for unsanctioned violence within the tribe must always be the threat of violence sanctioned by the group, because without any threat of violent reprisal, the strongest and most violent individuals could simply take whatever they wanted and kill anyone who disagreed, without any consideration for the survival or prosperity of the group as a whole. The tribe would collapse into chaos. Order demands violence — or the threat of it.

However, as with fair play, there is no guarantee or even a good reason to assume that if you make a commitment to live "non-violently" as an individual or a group, others will not take advantage of your pacifism and use violent means to destroy or enslave you to further their own interests. Choosing a path of non-aggression doesn't mean others aren't training to murder you and take your stuff. It is smarter to assume that they are, and plan accordingly.

As I noted in The Way of Men, humans and chimpanzees are "party-gang" species, meaning they can shift their allegiances from small groups to larger groups, based on social compatibility and the relative availability of resources. In times of scarcity, the perimeter of the group retracts to levels where trust can be consistently maintained between individual members — most often small, patriarchal gangs or tribes. It is also known that, generally speaking, allegiance to larger groups becomes increasingly abstract and tenuous and becomes more of a social performance as the size of the group expands, and that allegiance can only be maintained for any length of time through coercion, contract, substantial material incentives, a phenomenally strong common cultural identity or an impending existential threat posed by a common enemy. When there is a superordinate threat or goal, humans naturally break into smaller groups that can better serve their immediate interests and respond to their immediate concerns. They shift moral gears, and old allies become enemies battling for survival.

Those considered "barbarians" throughout history were not people without morality or codes of good and bad behavior. They were merely separate groups who took care of their own. Like all groups, including the "civilized" groups who called them barbarians, they were able to shift between different moral gears. They had one gear for insiders, and another gear for outsiders.

It will be said that I am advising men to abandon morality, but nothing could be further from the truth. Becoming a barbarian means abandoning the universalist morality that benefits the Empire for a specific morality that benefits a specific people and elevates the needs of those people over the needs of all outsiders.

This is not as simple as exchanging "slave morality" for "master morality" in the Nietzschean sense. It is true that the moral system promoted within the Empire is an heir to slave moralities. The Empire of Nothing certainly encourages expressions of ressentiment among "the oppressed" and theatrical self-flagellation among the successful. And its aim is certainly to create a master class of undeniably crafty but insufferably bitchy Mandarins, who rule a self-denying herd of impotent drone worker-consumers. The barbarian spirit, is by contrast, and indeed in Nietzsche's own words, maintained at the center of all the noblest, aristocratic-chivalric peoples, who base their value judgements on, "...a powerful physicality, a blossoming, rich, even effervescent good health that includes all of the things needed to maintain it, war, adventure, hunting, dancing, jousting and everything else that contains strong, free, happy action." Barbarians are alive in the world and say "yes!" to life. Barbarians live like beasts, without self-hatred or the need to apologize for living life at the expense of life, as all creatures do in some way or other.

However all tribes require collective cooperation and sympathy for those within that perimeter that separates "us" from "them." It seems likely that any functional group of humans would appreciate the value of charity, humility, sympathy and kindness when directed inward, to benefit "us." Masculine *thumos*, that spiritedness that drives the guardians to protect and to fight injustice and disorder, seems almost impossible without some sense of sympathy or charity toward less able members of the tribe. It is when the tactical virtues become subordinate to the "civilized" virtues in the cultural mainstream that a crippling, energy-sapping weakness overcomes a people and makes them easy to enslave with webs of petty rules and encourages submissive obsessions with comfort and etiquette. Theatrical gestures of kindness, charity and deference replace bold demonstrations of strength and courage, until legitimate strength and courage become morally suspect, and strength and courage must be charitably redefined to avoid hurting anyone's feelings. This elevation of naturally subordinate virtues and the consequent failure of virility at least partially explain the mass delusion seen today, where combat veterans are called cowards while transsexuals and morbidly obese women who do nude photo spreads are applauded as heroes.

An attachment to these "nicer," more sentimental virtues chains many otherwise virile men to a culture of weakness, and even motivates them to defend it, because they mistakenly view its abandonment as the abandonment of all that is good and decent in the world. These men who are good at being men, and who also want to be "good" men are exactly the kind of men you'd want in your tribe, but they are used, betrayed and played for fools by a culture that despises their strength and courage. While the Empire of the slave-mind manufactures more and more weakness for them to protect, their charges are ingrates, and they become martyrs to an ideal respected by almost no one but those who have served in their own ranks. Their tactical virtues are employed not to defend fragile beauty, but to spread a corpulent culture of ressentiment, material greed, weakness and hideous degeneracy across the globe. Progressively, as threats to security wane, they will be turned on each other and their nobility will be wasted defending the newfangled "rights" of the worst and weakest people to become as grotesque as possible. These pig people of Bartertown, who shamelessly luxuriate in their own filth and want to be told they are special for doing it, make the perfect corporate consumers to feed the methane-fueled furnaces of the global economy.

The best qualities of the best men, the men with the most heroic potential, are being wasted by manipulators who have convinced them that they can't be "good" men unless they do what is best for everyone, everywhere. This is impossible, so elites gin up reasons why men must fight, not for "us," but to somehow save the world from evil. It just so happens that what is deemed universally good generally tends to open up new markets, increase access to natural resources, or resolve conflicts that interrupt the flow of international commerce. The immediate impact of the influence of these heroic sacrifices appears to be an increase in wealth and quality of life for people living in the affected regions, but the long-term reality of successful interventions is always a loss of identity, loss of meaningful self-determination, the consolidation of global wealth into the hands of elites, and the conversion of virile men and warriors into worker-consumer drones.

To escape this exploitation, men must recognize the lie of universal good for what it is — a story for slaves.

There is no saving the world, and the world isn't your responsibility anyway. You are not a god! What a haughty fantasy — that the fate of all mankind hinges on the axis of your resolve!

When someone says "we all have a responsibility" to do something, they are just trying to talk you into doing what they want for their own selfish reasons, or to sign onto their vain and delusional Quixote quest. The truth is that it probably doesn't matter what you do. At the scale of billions, in all but the rarest of instances, your actions will do nothing to change the fate of humanity. Your vote, your service, your charity, your purchases, your sorting of recyclables, your precious opinions — your life and your death — are all pin drops in a parade.

However, if you recalibrate the scope of your responsibility from the infinite to the finite, your actions are more likely to be important. If you are responsible for and accountable to a smaller group, everything you do and all of your choices are mathematically far more meaningful.

There is no need to abandon kindness, generosity, sympathy, honesty, humility or even The Golden Rule. There is no need to abandon all moral responsibility to others. You can still be a good man, but you can't be equally good to everyone. And if you do not choose who you will be good for and to, your choices will be made for you by others, for reasons of their own, or they may even end up being more or less arbitrary.

Those who have drawn or accepted the boundaries of their moral responsibilities are not immoral, but they will necessarily have at least two moral gears. There is what is best for "us," and what is good enough for "them" — there is a distinction between intra-tribal morality and inter-tribal morality.

Intra-tribal morality concerns one's moral responsibility to and within the tribe, for the good of the tribe.

Inter-tribal morality concerns one tribe's relationship with another tribe, and one's moral responsibility to members of another tribe or to an outsider of unknown tribal affiliation.

Humans have been operating this moral gear shift adeptly throughout human history. It isn't inhuman — it's *exactly* human. It allows men to shift dynamically from caring loyally and consistently for those close to them to killing outsiders with no remorse when necessary. A commitment to treating everyone equally as if they were part of your tribe or family and assuming that they have made a similar commitment invites exploitation. It turns you into the naive country boy bound to get bamboozled in the big city. The universalist approach clouds perception, because humans don't think or work that way. Strangers will generally favor their own interests and the interests of their people, no matter what they say. Watching what they do allows you to see the world clearly, and make the best decisions for yourself and your tribe.

"Endeavor to not waste time in the company, or trying to change the minds, of those content with spinning their wheels and flapping their gums.

Instead, use the time and energy to move further forward... The more you progress, the more they'll stew, and the more you learn, the less they'll do..."

— Greg Walsh, *Wolf Brigade.com*

NO APOLOGIES.
NO ARGUMENTS.
NO EXPLANATIONS.

Why explain yourself to strangers — or worse — your enemies? Why try to convince them of anything? Why argue or debate with outsiders? What is to be gained from this kind of exchange?

Offering an explanation for your words, thoughts or actions to outsiders or enemies is defensive, or at best, strategically passive-aggressive.

Explaining or defending your actions, thoughts or words to your brothers or members of your tribe is a demonstration of loyalty and respect. If you have been accused of behaving badly, or in a manner inconsistent with your tribal culture, you explain and defend yourself because you want to remain a part of that tribe and maintain or regain the respect of your peers.

This is an *apologia*, in the original sense of the word. Apologetics is a branch of Christian theology concerned with the defending or explaining the faith to non-Christian critics, although other religions and philosophies have employed similar strategies when interacting with outsiders.

Apologetics comes from the Latin *apologeticus*, which in turn comes from the Greek apologetikos. In the Ancient Greek legal system, when charges were brought against you in court, you responded with an apologia — a formal "apology" or "defence".

If you have not been accused of any misdeed, but simply wish others in your tribe to consider a course of action at your recommendation, it is productive to defend and engage in a debate concerning the merits of your idea. Likewise, if you object to a suggested course of action, you show a man respect by hearing his idea and attempting to convince him that he is mistaken.

A man engages in apologetics or sincere debate intra-tribally because he cares. He cares about the direction of the tribe and the prosperity of his people. He argues because he cares about whether or not his tribe respects and values him. He argues to protect, defend or increase his honor within the group.

Men develop and establish formal rules and etiquette for argumentation and the resolution of disagreements to maintain civility and unity within a given tribe. Any group, from the largest to the smallest, will eventually have competing factions of men pressing different agendas and ideas. These factions argue because they care about the survival, prosperity and culture of the group as a whole. Or, as is often the case, especially in larger political systems, the factions formally maintain the pretense of friendly argumentation while ruthlessly sabotaging each other.

Competing political parties always argue from the starting assumption that what they want is best for the nation as a whole. They may despise their opponents more than foreign enemies, or they may merely be serving personal interests at the expense of any ideology at all, but to abandon the pretense that they want what is best for the country would be completely taboo — because it would undermine the overarching identity of the tribe or expose them as corrupt and self-interested charlatans.

Men argue, debate and explain their positions intra-tribally within a conceptual framework that presupposes tribal unity, mutual respect, shared identity and wanting what is best for the tribe as a whole.

This manner of debate and argumentation is the habit, or at least the acknowledged ideal, of most Western men. It has a long tradition in the West, reaching back to the Classical era, and it is the style of argumentation we have all been taught and which is expected of us in any forum. It works, and the conventions of Western argumentation are productive — within a unified group or tribe.

Like most Western conventions that survived because they were highly functional for smaller groups of men, civilized debate and argumentation leads to impotence, corruption and indecision when applied universally. It remains useful in the hard sciences, where proofs can be offered and examined objectively by anyone with the intelligence to comprehend and process the evidence and arguments being presented. However, Western-style debate and argumentation becomes wasteful and even harmful when its basic assumption — that everyone involved shares an identity, a common culture, and ultimately wants what is best for the group — is untrue. Politics becomes even more of a magnet for self-aggrandizing sociopaths and liars than it already tends to be by nature, and men with no meaningful political power or authority waste their time and energy trying to convince complete strangers to convert to their way of thinking, even when those strangers have different group identities, different religious beliefs, and completely incompatible or opposing ideas about what is good or "best in life."

The Universalist man, as an egalitarian citizen of the Empire and member of the One True Human Tribe, has accepted the responsibility of somehow convincing an infinite amount of people that his actions are in the interest of everyone, everywhere and that he wants what is best for everyone, everywhere, even if they are openly hostile to him and do not consider themselves part of his One True Tribe. This cannot even be described as a Sisyphean task, because it is non-linear.

Universalist man doesn't have to push a single boulder up a single hill — he has charged himself with pushing a functionally infinite number of boulders up an infinite number of hills. He has essentially made himself responsible for and accountable to every single living human — and some have gone so far as to claim responsibility for the welfare and happiness of animals, plants and the entire Earth as well. The Universalist man accepts responsibilities that could only be fulfilled by an omniscient god. As such, he is both obnoxious and a failure.

This implied responsibility for a man to consider everyone, everywhere's opinion and bring everyone, everywhere around to his opinion is illustrated millions of times every day all over the Internet and social media. Men engage in pointless and never-ending arguments with complete strangers — who are often anonymous and questionably sincere — as if they were their brothers, friends, or next-door neighbors. By involving himself in arguments with strangers, a man opens himself up to an infinite number of challenges from other men or women who then feel entitled to a response, as a tribal brother, friend or peer would rightfully feel entitled to a response.

Many young men who have grown up on the Internet see these debates as a cathartic game of one-upmanship, and troll discussions purely for the satisfaction of catching someone in a confused or emotional response. Like hackers, they often like to pretend they are providing some kind of service, but this is rationalization, as they generally troll out of boredom, not selfless nobility. So, by engaging in these sorts of arguments, a man not only opens himself up to sincere challenges from strangers, outsiders and others with completely different interests and values, he opens himself up to insincere attacks motivated merely by the boredom of hecklers.

Video games and vicarious obsessions like spectator sports and pornography are frequently blamed for diverting the attentions and energies of men away from meaningful, first-person pursuits and live action in "meatspace," but these online debates with strangers may waste just as much of the time and effort of able-bodied, intelligent and talented men. Debate for the sake of debate is an intellectualized form of masculine competition in a world badly in need of visceral, direct masculinity.

The Universalist Man must argue with and defend his ideas and actions to everyone, everywhere because he accepts everyone, everywhere as part of his tribe. He considers it barbaric to disregard the opinions or interests of anyone, anywhere.

The Barbarian refuses to accept everyone, everywhere as a member of his tribe. Because he is not blinded by a doctrine of infinite inclusiveness, he recognizes that others have interests and values that are irreconcilable with his own. He is beholden to a limited number of people — to "us" — and owes no explanation or justification to "them." Contemplate the absurdity of a Viking explaining to monks why he is "right" to attack their monastery, or Attilla justifying his attacks on the Roman Empire to anyone but the Huns. Power makes its own argument.

Explanations and apologies to outsiders are the issue of flaccid, failing and feminine cultures.

There are, of course, exceptions.

There are tactical reasons for explanations, arguments and apologies. If you are part of a minority group, for instance, you may want to engage in some sort of strategic apologetics.

Various religions, including Christianity, have developed apologetics to make their presence seem tolerable to outsiders in areas where they were a minority influence. Jews argue from the perspective of being "part" of a larger community even when they ultimately see themselves as being distinct and separate from that community. Muslims manipulate Western moderates by appealing for tolerance and understanding in public forums, even as they preach intolerance in their mosques. This approach exploits the cultural weakness of the dominant culture in a region to create space for the expansion and empowerment of the minority culture. Tactical explanations, arguments and apologies may be duplicitous or riddled with half-truths, because truth is owed only internally. Tactical explanations, arguments and apologies are tools designed to accomplish a purpose.

There is some danger though, in the potential for the tactical rationale offered to outsiders to infect the culture of insiders and muddle their perception of themselves. In trying to convince others that they are harmless and should be left alone so that members aren't harassed or persecuted, actually become harmless and indistinguishable from dominant cultures in terms of their everyday beliefs. This is true of the majority of "alternative" religious groups today.

Another reason to engage in apologetics is to facilitate conversion. The evangelical Universalist must theoretically be willing to "share the good word" with everyone, everywhere, but the tribalist only seeks to convert or recruit desirable individuals — those whose conversion or recruitment would ultimately benefit the tribe or group in some way. The tribalist should be able to address the concerns of those interested in recruitment or conversion, and be able to distinguish what "we" believe or how "we" live from what "they" believe and how "they" live.

Along similar lines, a tribalist might develop an explanation or argument for his tribal culture to act as a beacon to attract "the right kind of people." This is one reason a man might write a book, for instance.

Beyond this strategic kind of apologetics, there are few reasons to engage tribal outsiders or ideological opponents in debate or attempt to convince them of anything.

If you are motivated by some hope that things would be better if everyone, everywhere would just agree to alter their thoughts or actions in a particular way, you are already and will always be wrong. People will always have different interests and agendas, and arguing as if you could conceivably convince everyone of anything is a masturbatory exercise.

Argumentation is wasted on enemies and strangers. Arguing is something you should do with people who you know and respect, because you want what is best for them and for you, and because their opinion matters to you. Argue within your circle.

Fuck everyone else.

"...hunting and fighting are both of the same general character. Both are of a predatory nature; the warrior and the hunter alike reap where they have not strewn. Their aggressive assertion of force and sagacity differs obviously from the women's assiduous and uneventful shaping of materials; it is not to be accounted productive labour, but rather an acquisition of substance by seizure. Such being the barbarian man's work, in its best development and widest divergence from women's work, any effort that does not involve an assertion of prowess comes to be unworthy of the man."

"When the predatory habit of life has been settled upon the group by long habituation, it becomes the able-bodied man's accredited office in the social economy to kill, to destroy such competitors in the struggle for existence as attempt to resist or elude him, to overcome and reduce to subservience those alien forces that assert themselves refractorily in the environment."

— Thorstein Veblen, *The Theory of the Leisure Class*

LOOT, PILLAGE AND PLUNDER

To become a barbarian in this age, you must leave the Empire behind spiritually, but you can never escape it materially. Its infrared cameras will find you in whatever Siberian lean-to you flee to. The Empire is everywhere. Every word and idea in this book passed through its channels.

However, suppose that one could escape the leviathan and all of its wriggling tentacles. What would be achieved? Some abstract purity of your precious, individual and unsullied soul? What is the point of scrubbing its filth from your nails and refusing its bounty? Would you feel better, superior to all of those money-grubbing, celebrity-worshiping, consumer drones if you manage to bathe yourself clean of their influences? Would you not simply be delaying the inevitable for yourself and your friends by saying "no" over and over again to every modern thing?

An obsession with purity is the sickness of priests and the hypocrisy of parasites. Asceticism and retreat are resignation, not revolt.

To become a barbarian in this age is to defiantly pitch an identity and stand against an insatiable commercial organism that devours all identities and excretes a formless pudding of monocultural mediocrity.

Barbarians say "yes" to life. They take what they want from the Empire and leave the rest to rot. They are alive without apology, bold and willing to fight for and seize what they want and what they need for them and theirs. Because anyone outside the tribe is no one to them, when they take, they take from no one. They will wear necklaces of your teeth — not to luxuriate in their own cruelty — but to celebrate their own victory over death, weakness and failure. Barbarians know that living is always taking. They have freed themselves from delusion and know who and what they are.

The civilized man is either tormented by guilt, or he pretends to be tormented to display his superior morality and thereby increase or maintain his social status. He has inherited the doctrine of original sin, internalized it and secularized it to the point where his original sin is living. He wants to erase his footprints and apologize for every advantage and talent. He is concerned with fairness, though life has never been fair, and gives away power and privilege to anyone who accuses him of having it or who feels somehow disadvantaged. Because he is responsible to everyone, there will always be someone worse off to defer and apologize to.

The civilized man worries not only about his actions, but about his words and even his daydreams. He dares not think unfair thoughts. This guilt for living makes him easy to control. It makes him weak, because it makes him fear his own strength. He has confused this weakness with nobility, imagining himself a white knight, but everyone else sees him as an easy mark. He is afraid to take, so others happily take from him.

This concern for the feelings of others is an intertribal perversion of his intratribal moral sensibility. To take only what you need and share freely with others is a practical, mutually beneficial practice within a tribe of connected and interdependent people. Giving freely encourages goodwill and the return of favors. Relaxed deference to others in matters of no particular import — like holding a door open, for instance — demonstrates an easy vitality and strengthens social bonds. It acknowledges that, "we are all in this together." However, in a world of strangers, there are no social bonds to strengthen. Men go through the motions of building community where no true community or cultural connectedness exists beyond something flimsy, like "we are humans who inhabit the same general geographical area." Their good efforts are more often than not empty, wasted gestures.

Unprovoked hostility to strangers is always fun but usually tactically foolish. Pointless hostility draws attention and encourages reciprocated hostility. Assholes who run into trouble all the time probably run into trouble because they are assholes. There is no reason to be rude, and some adherence to popular social customs — like holding a door open, for instance — is smart. A reputation for rudeness is not the same as a reputation for strength.

However, becoming a barbarian means being willing to take ruthlessly from others when necessary or advantageous. A barbarian is ready to plunder for him and his. Unfairness and the feelings of outsiders can be of no more concern than the feelings of a slaughtered pig. What matters is the bacon.

To become a barbarian, the civilized man must realize that even if he took from nothing from anyone and treated everyone, everywhere with absolute fairness, this would not guarantee that others would reciprocate and refuse to take from him or treat him unfairly. In all likelihood, his commitment to selflessness will attract people eager to exploit him.

Take, or be taken from.

There are consequences for taking. Laws of the land must be considered — not as moral guidelines, but as physical risk factors.

There may also, in some cases, be a threat of immediate or delayed reprisal.

However, many systems and policies rely on a collective sense of moral responsibility that invites and rewards exploitation by those who do not share that collective sense of moral responsibility. Millions of people, if not most people, are already gaming some system or another — from stockbrokers to small business owners to women who know which stores have the "no questions asked" return policies. If there is a loophole in some rule or some "good faith" policy, someone is out there exploiting it.

Why isn't it you?

No publicly traded company will ever love you or care what happens to you. They are self-perpetuating legal entities whose sole purpose is to generate profit. Treating them "fairly," and dealing with them "in good faith" as if they were the local plumber you went to school with is pure foolishness. If they make it easy to take from them, do it for you and yours. A publicly traded corporation's feelings can't get hurt, because such corporations have no feelings. Exploit their loopholes until they are closed, or until you've bled them dry.

It makes sense to give greater consideration to smaller, privately-owned businesses, especially if they are local or if they produce something of value to you. Considerate exchanges may help build your support network. For years I've been an advocate of "hating globally and 'liking' locally." Outlaw gangs or extremist groups often win public support or sympathy in their area by cultivating positive business relationships and helping people. It's hard for people to hate the guys who come into their businesses smiling, politely buying their goods and tipping well. However, if some business owner is a jerk, an enemy or a threat to your interests, fuck him. What's "fair" is irrelevant. You owe him nothing.

Not my people, not my problem.

The state — the Empire of Nothing — is essentially a collection of self-perpetuating bureaucratic organizations. The state sees you as a number, a demographic, a tax bracket, a potential violator of law to be dealt with "impartially." To the politicians who direct the operations of the state you are a vote, a poll number, a donor — possibly even an enemy or a threat. In theory, the government of the United States of America exists to protect the bodies, rights and interests of American citizens. All 300 million or so of them. In reality, politicians legislate to protect their biggest donors, the special interest groups that get them elected, and people to whom they owe favors. The state itself may theoretically exist to protect national interests — the interests of its people as a whole — but the adoption of universalist morality has blurred the line between citizens of the state and "citizens of the world." The US and the governments in Europe which are also stricken with universal morality have welcomed the export of jobs, the import of unskilled immigrants and hostile refugees, and they have engaged their citizens in costly foreign wars that offer little or no benefit or protection to average citizens.

The state does not serve your interests. It serves its own. As the largest of large corporations whose interests are protected and enforced by the largest of gangs, the state will extort as much money and labor from you as it can within the limits it sets for itself to maintain a minimum level of public support and a maximum level of compliance. It does not, and cannot love you or care what happens to you. The state is not your friend, or your mom, or your dad. It does not worry about you or respect you or appreciate your contribution. When the state "gives" you something, whether it is a commendation or a welfare check, it does so largely for the theater of public relations.

For instance, while writing this, I was summoned to attend jury duty. Throughout the jury selection process, coordinators and judges reminded us how important our presence was, and how deeply they and the State of Oregon appreciated our service. The Chief Justice of the Supreme Court of Oregon and several judges who may or may not have been actors thanked us via video. The big joke of it was that attending jury service is mandatory and my summons threatened me with the possibility of being held in contempt of court for non-compliance. That pretty much sums up how the state "appreciates" its citizens.

"We thank you very much for your mandatory attendance."

It's like thanking prisoners for staying in jail.

You can get as choked up as you want over national anthems and stock video footage of flags billowing proudly in the wind, but the modern state is a machine run by millions of individuals making career decisions that serve their own immediate self-interests.

The state is a self-perpetuating system operated by managers who are unlikely to decide on their own to close their departments and fire all of their employees, no matter how absurd, redundant or intrusive their departments become. To keep their jobs and advance their own interests, they will naturally seek out ways to rationalize and justify their work to themselves and to their superiors. They will occasionally be checked and reorganized in response to budgetary concerns or public backlash, again, to maintain a minimum level of public support and a maximum level of compliance.

Some good friends of mine currently live across the street from a welfare office — or human services department, whatever they are calling it these days. As these guys get ready to go to work every morning, they sneer at the line of ne'er-do-wells lining up for their handouts. My friends are viscerally disgusted by the parade of open hands, of men and women who could work like they are working, but who choose not to. It makes them angry. Why should they work and pay taxes while these seemingly able-bodied men spend an hour in line and then stroll home to lives of leisure? No man wants to go drive a forklift in the middle of the night for somebody else's construction project. No man wants to spend all day washing dishes or working in the wet cold cleaning out somebody else's ship. My friends go to work because they are proud and decent men who believe that a man should carry his own weight in life.

Their instincts are good, which is why they are the kind of men who I want in my tribe.

In any functional tribe, every man should be expected to carry his own weight — at the very least. A successful and respected man also helps carry the weight of some others. He doesn't merely survive, he produces some kind of surplus, some kind of prosperity that can be shared by others within the perimeter of the group. He works to support not only himself, but the women and children and truly infirm or disabled. Every true leader of men I know feels a strong sense of responsibility to those who depend on the surplus he generates, and this sense of responsibility motivates him to work harder, to produce more and thereby increase prosperity and quality of life for his friends, his people, and his family. A good man in any tribe shares the bounty yielded by his strength.

This desire to work to carry your own weight and help carry the weight of others is the vestige of functional intratribal morality.

But, as is often the case when intratribal morality is extended intertribally, the functional becomes dysfunctional. It is the "good men" who are exploited by both the lazy and those who have recognized that the game has changed.

My friends are still, in some sense, morally evaluating the freeloaders as they would evaluate members of their own tribe. They are judging "them" — these strangers in line — as if they were "us." They see the healthy welfare recipients as parasites who take and give nothing back. And in some abstract way, my friends are still identifying themselves with the Empire. After all, they pay taxes — albeit non-voluntarily — so a fraction of the surplus of their own labor is theoretically being doled out to men who refuse to work. They see the resources of the state, of the Empire of Nothing, as *their* resources. These "good men" would feel ashamed — dishonored — if they went begging to the State, to take what they had not earned by the work of their own hands, to have their weight carried by other men who are no more able. So they work, and continue to support the very system they despise.

I make my own living and pay taxes, as I have for my entire adult life. I have never taken welfare or even managed to get an unemployment check. I have probably given far more to the state than it has given to me over the years. I can only think of a handful of times when I have received any specific benefits from the state at all, beyond benefitting as we all do from the general order maintained by policing and the use of public works projects like roads.

I have no plans to personally apply for any kind of assistance from the state, but I no longer have any animosity toward men who do. I no longer see the state's resources as my own. Actually, I see state funds as money that has been extorted from me incrementally over nearly two decades and I'd be happy to see the surplus of my labor returned to me in any way possible.

But even if I had never paid taxes, I'd still take the government's money.

The Empire isn't my tribe. The government isn't my people.

I would be disgusted by any man in my in my own tribe if he constantly took from the group and gave nothing in return. But if the same man were taking from the Empire so that he could give more to the tribe, he'd have my respect.

Men today suffer so acutely from the affliction of universal morality that many feel obligated to not only treat every stranger as they'd wish to be treated, but also to treat governments and corporations as they themselves would wish to be treated.

Rest assured, no state or publicly traded corporation is comparably impaired. Governments and companies want you to identify with them and morally anthropomorphize them so that you will buy their products, follow their rules and contribute to their institutional survival. They cultivate an allegiance in the flesh, because it is cheaper and often more reliable than imposing order with steel. Or lead.

Refusing to accept the abundance made available to you by states and corporations will not change the world. It will not change their policies and it will probably not influence any strangers to change their way of life.

Some might argue that, "If everyone did [blank], then [blank] would happen." But this is universalist thinking. You are not personally responsible for the actions of "everyone," and your actions will probably not influence the actions of "everyone" in any measurable way.

Your actions are your own, and while they have little influence on the world, they could make a substantial impact on your tribe and the people you care about. You're not going to stop globalism by refusing to buy things from big corporations, and you're not going to change social assistance programs by refusing to take what is offered, but you could potentially save money that you could then invest in the prosperity of your tribe.

There is no escape from the Empire, so you can either choose to be proud and allow the Empire to exploit you and do nothing, or you can choose to exploit the Empire in return and improve the prospects of your people.

Some will inevitably call you a hypocrite for disparaging the Empire even as you benefit from its prosperity, networks and technology — implying that you should reject all things tainted by the establishment you despise. Even if you lived "off the grid" as a hermit, you would probably benefit in some way from the existence of the Empire. Denying yourself and your people the tools and resources that everyone else has at their disposal only insures that you and your people will be at a disadvantage and will be unable to compete with other groups. Imagine how easy it would be to slaughter the horde of barbarians that spurned the use of weapons due to some perceived "impurity." How easy would it be to rip off someone who refuses to learn math or out-compete a businessman who won't use a computer?

Absolute purity only guarantees poverty, vulnerability or irrelevance. The best outcome you could hope for would be to become a quaint sideshow for gawking tourists — like the Amish. And even that is unlikely.

Instead of engaging yourself in the Sisyphean, self-defeating and self-denying task of purifying yourself from the Empire, use The Moral Gear Shift. Decide what values are important to you and your tribe and maintain them within the social perimeter of the group, but employ whatever means are necessary to ensure the tribe's survival and prosperity in the context of the world as it exists in the present — not as you wish it to be in the future or imagine it was in the past.

Accept every advantage. Exploit every opportunity. Exhaust every resource. Take everything the modern world has to offer and use it to aid your revolt and improve the future prospects of your people.

Do not think like a citizen of the bloated Empire. Imagine yourself beyond the walls of Rome, and see its abundance beckoning from afar, as a barbarian would.

Given the opportunity, what would you loot, pillage and plunder?

And...given the opportunity — why *wouldn't* you?

"He who breaks the law has gone to war with the community; the community goes to war with him. It is the right and duty of every man to pursue him, to ravage his land, to burn his house, to hunt him down like a wild beast and slay him; for a wild beast he is; not merely is he a 'friendless man,' he is a wolf. Even in the Thirteenth Century, when outlawry had lost its exterminating character and become an engine for compelling the contumacious to abide the judgement of the courts, the old state of things was not forgotten: Caput gerat lupinum — in these words the courts decreed outlawry."

— Sir Frederick Pollock
& Frederic William Maitland
The History of English Law
Before the Time of Edward I.

CAPUT GERAT LUPINUM

No good, modern, civilized man wants to think of himself as a "criminal." Most men see themselves as "good guys."

Men with a taste or talent for violence who want to be "good guys" often refer to themselves as "sheepdogs" — a metaphor popularized by Lt. Col. Dave Grossman in his book *On Combat*. According to Grossman, a sheepdog has a deep love for and fights to protect sheep, defined as "healthy, productive citizens" with "no capacity for violence," from wolves, who have a capacity for violence but "no empathy for [their] fellow citizens." Grossman diagnoses wolves as "aggressive sociopaths."[1]

These definitions are far too simple...too black and white.

The ideal of the sheepdog conjures the traditional role of men, who have always been expected to fight to protect everyone and everything inside the perimeter of their tribe against threats from outside that perimeter, whether those threats come from nature or or from other groups of men.

However, when there is danger afoot, *every man* will be expected by women and children and other men to protect the perimeter — not just a few officially appointed "sheepdogs." Despite Grossman's

1   Grossman's essay "On Sheep, Wolves and Sheepdogs" is currently available online at http://killology.com/sheep_dog.htm

assurances, telling the majority of men that they either have "no capacity for violence" is both insulting and inaccurate.

Grossman's sheepdogs — cops and soldiers and some first responders — have simply applied for permission to do violence on behalf of the state. The number of these jobs or "permits" available is extremely limited, and there are many rational reasons not to apply for them beyond having "no capacity for violence." If every man who was able to play sheepdog applied to play sheepdog, only a tiny percentage could be permitted to play sheepdog. Further, only a tiny percentage of men who enlist in the military hoping to fight will ever see combat, and many policemen hand out tickets for years or even entire careers without drawing their weapons.

Those who do become the state's sheepdogs may never get a chance to tangle with wolves, but one of their primary purposes is to intimidate the sheep enough that they don't become wolves. The qualities that differentiate "criminals" from "sheep" are not necessarily sociopathy or a propensity for violence, but impulse control and a rational fear of state authority. Most men recognize that executing "unauthorized violence" will result in them being designated as outlaws, hunted down by sheepdogs, threatened with state-authorized violence, and then either killed or imprisoned. The modern legal system didn't evolve to protect innocent Hobbit-like sheeple from psycho-killer-wolves. It evolved in part to keep average men from killing each other over slights and getting involved in never-ending cycles of blood-feuds. The sheepdogs have permission to use violence to maintain the state's monopoly on violence.

The state's agents of authorized violence may believe that they are serving and protecting, and they are doing that too, but like the mob, if you don't pay them tribute and follow their rules, you may well find yourself a victim of their violence. Or a "volunteer," if you prefer.

Plato referred to his guardian class, his sheepdogs, as "noble puppies." I've borrowed that phrase many times myself — but aren't puppies and sheepdogs both a bit too cute? Perhaps even insulting? Would ancient warriors have wanted to be called "puppies" or "sheepdogs?"

What is a sheepdog if not a domesticated wolf who, as the result of his breeding, training, and conditioning, does exactly what he is told?

A sheepdog is a pet. A sheepdog has a master. His master owns him. The sheepdog's master is not the sheep. His master uses the sheepdog to control the sheep, who are his assets with which he will do as he pleases.

Agent Clarice Starling, a sheepdog herself, knows what happens to the spring lambs.

One wonders if these so-called "sheepdogs" will ever wake up screaming, knowing they aided in the slaughter of their charges, or if they will simply block it out and move on, barking…

"…the wolves…the wolves…the wolves are coming…"

Perhaps a "sheepdog," then, isn't such a noble thing to be after all.

And being the sheep of a man who imagines himself as a sheepdog isn't so great, either. The "sheep" metaphor is rarely used mean anything but "helpless dumb sucker."

If men are loyal to your tribe, and they are willing to maim and murder other men to protect you, why insult them by calling them slavish, domesticated pets? Why not call them *your* wolves? Don't wolves defend their own pack?

If you are fighting to protect people you care about — your people — then why fight like a sheepdog when you can fight like a wolf?

Dispense with the fairy tale morality and join the rest of us in the grown-up world where we don't have to pretend someone fighting for our team is fighting for universal good against universal evil — as long as they are fighting for *us*.

This real life, not a comic book movie. No one is fighting an intergalactic alien death squad. They're just fighting other men who are fighting for their people or their interests or their masters. Even if they were fighting aliens or reptilians or giants, would it really be about good versus evil, or just another conflict between us and them?

If you move from Hollywood's Thor to studying what actually remains of the old lore, you will come to understand that Loki and the giants aren't evil — they are forces of chaos and change. They present challenges to be overcome.

In Old Norse, that which is inside the perimeter of protection is called *innangarðr*, or "within the enclosure." Innangarðr describes the space of ordered violence defined by the boundaries of identity. Innangarðr is "us," and medieval Icelanders described their society itself as "*vár lög*" or "our law." That which was beyond the reach of the law and therefore disordered and chaotic, that which was beyond the protected perimeter and outside the enclosure was known as *útangarðr*.

One of the names for the realm of the giants was *Útgarðr*, meaning essentially the same thing as útangarðr — outside the perimeter of protection. *Ásgarðr* was the realm of the gods, or Aesir, and they symbolized what is often referred to as solar, uranic, apollonian or ordered, harmonious and restrained world. Gods like Thor and Tyr and Odin fought to keep the giants or *jötnar*, out of Ásgarðr and to protect humans in *Miðgarðr* (the middle enclosure) from the mischief of the jötnar. Among the jötnar were frost giants and fire giants as well as Loki and his children: Fenrir the wolf, Jörmungandr the world-encircling serpent and Hel, the mistress of the world of the dead.

However, the gods themselves were often part jötunn. They bargained and played games with the jötnar as often as they fought with them, and they even fell in love with and mated with them. The jötnar weren't evil, they were just different creatures with interests and natures of their own. When their interests conflicted with the interests of gods or men, they simply needed to be dealt with. They were a "thorn in the side" for gods and men. In fact, another name for jötnar was *þursar*, meaning both "powerful and injurious" and "thorn-like." Others have associated þursar with a root for "thirst", implying bloodthirst, and jötnar comes from a root that means "devourer."[2]

The þursar and jötnar were bloodthirsty, devouring creatures from útangarðr — outside the enclosure of order. Þursar were thorns to men and gods, threatening to derail or destroy everything they had built. They were uncontrollable forces of nature, like storms, fires, bears, earthquakes...perhaps even wolves. They weren't good or evil, but they were threats to those who were innangardr, or within the circle.

There are two ways to look at threats from outside the circle. You can accept them as challenges to be overcome and opportunities for greatness and glory — which is what Thor would do — or you can be low test about it and see it as evil meanies picking on you and

---

2   This segment draws from and was inspired by Dan McCoy's pithy explanations of Germanic concepts at norse-mythology.org, specifically
http://norse-mythology.org/concepts/innangard-and-utangard/

your friends. A world without strife is a world without glory. Life is conflict; peace is death. Forces of chaos keep the cycles of history moving.

You don't have to literally believe in gods or giants to recognize the timeless human truth of this metaphorical model. It's another way to make sense of the role of men in society, of law and lawlessness, of order and chaos, of insiders and outsiders — of "us" vs. "them."

One of the reasons that "good guys" don't want to see themselves as wolves is that our ancestors saw wolves as wild, external forces of chaos. Wolves lived outside the enclosure of the town or village and preyed on lost, helpless and untended animals — and sometimes even humans. Little Red Riding Hood got eaten because she was tricked by an outsider, a wolf, who encouraged her to dawdle in the dark woods and wander off the path to grandmas on her way through the forest of the unknown. Wolves were devourerers, always hungry. The wolves Sköll and Hati chased the sun and the moon across the sky, trying to swallow them. Even Odin himself was destined to be killed by the giant wolf Fenrir. But he was also associated with wolves, because hungry wolves are scavengers, like eagles, and after a battle they were often seen feasting on the corpses of the slain. To triumph in battle was to give one's enemy to the wolves, and to prospect of defeat meant becoming food for the wolves and the eagles and the ravens.

In smaller, more tribal communities, there were no professional executioners or hangmen. Only large cities had dedicated law enforcement officers. Men who were deemed a threat to order within the community, whether because due to murder or some other unforgivable act, were declared outlaws. Being an outlaw meant being outside the legal protection of the community, of vár lög. An outlaw was literally beyond the law, banished from innangarðr to útangarðr, sent out past the boundaries of the known, ordered world and into the disordered unknown where anything could happen. His property would be seized, and no one would consider it theft. He could be killed by anyone, and it would not be considered murder. No one would avenge him. The outlaw was stripped of all rights held by members of the community. He had no friends or family and basically became a non-person. He was completely dehumanized.

The Romans referred to an outlaw who could be killed by anyone with impunity as homo sacer, meaning that as a man he was set apart. It is from the Latin sacer that we get the word "sacred," but in this usage, it meant being set apart in the sense of being cursed. In Old Norse, the outlawed man was said to be "going to the forest," or skóggangr. This idea persisted, and throughout the Middle Ages, a man who was outlawed was said to "wear the head of a wolf" — *caput gerat lupinum.* He was no longer a man, but a wolf who could be hunted and killed by anyone like any wild animal.

Today, at least in most modern, civilized Western countries, only state-sanctioned agents of violence — the sheepdogs, or whatever you want to call them — are ever permitted to seize a man's property, hunt him down and kill him. So, there are no outlaws, in exactly the original sense. Even prisoners who have been condemned to death are allowed some legal rights. No one exists completely outside the system.

However, a transformation still occurs. A man who has been convicted of breaking the law becomes a "criminal." Everyone has broken some kind of law, and most people are breaking several at any given time, but what transforms the citizen into a criminal is getting caught. The people who were growing and dealing and smoking marijuana before it was legalized in some states and the people who are growing and dealing and smoking marijuana now in states where it hasn't been legalized are or have been involved in criminal activity. They are or were technically criminals, but no one refers to them as criminals until they are legally charged with crimes. Everyone who has ever downloaded a song or a movie illegally has committed a crime. Men can drink and drive, snort coke, bootleg, beat their wives, gamble, hire prostitutes, sell guns, use fake IDs, write bad checks, cheat on taxes, beat each other up and straight-up murder motherfuckers...but no one calls them criminals until they get caught doing it. As Whitey Bulger says in the movie *Black Mass* (2015):

"It's not what you do, it's when and where you do it. And who you do it to or with … If nobody sees it, it didn't happen."

However, if and when someone does see it, and you get caught — if you are charged and convicted and especially if you go to prison — then you become a different kind of person. A man who breaks the law is just a man, but a man who gets caught and goes to prison — he's a criminal. And, even after he has "done his time"... for many years afterward many people will refuse to hire him or rent to him. Most felons aren't allowed to vote, and just about every "don't tread on me," "hands off my guns" Second Amendment activist and talk show host agrees that criminals should never have legal access to guns. Because once a man is a criminal, he is a different kind of person. He's a *bad* person. He's no longer one of the good people who obeys "our law" inside the enclosed, ordered space. He may not be banished to the wilderness, and not just anyone is allowed to kill him or take his stuff, but he is not fully trusted. He is regarded as a potential force of chaos — wild, dangerous and unpredictable.

All kinds of men, even sheepdogs, commit crimes. There are all kind of different reasons why men commit crimes. Some men are certainly more inclined to break the law than others, and some men are more aggressive than others by nature. But a man is not a criminal until the government identifies him as a criminal, as a felon, as the lighter contemporary version of the man who wears the head of a wolf.

Criminal is a designation of the state, not necessarily a type of person. By getting caught or openly breaking the laws of the state, he undermines order within the borders of the enclosure. Without violence, laws are just words, so anyone who has been designated a criminal will find himself an enemy of the state.

"He who breaks the law has gone to war with the community; the community goes to war with him."

A criminal is regarded as a bad person, or different kind of person who must to a certain extent be dehumanized because people still allow the state to make moral determinations for them — as if modern governments represent the collective consensus of the people, the tribe, the village. The good, modern, civilized man doesn't want to be considered a criminal, and he treats known criminals like different kinds of people — bad, evil, throwaway people — because his moral orientation includes the assumption or belief that criminals have broken "our law."

This belief or assumption returns us to the fundamental questions and challenges of this book.

Who is "we?"

Who is "us?"

Who makes "our law?"

Who makes the law of the land?

Is it "us," or is it "them?"

If you are willing to accept that the law of the land is "our law," no matter what the laws are, no matter who the lawmakers are, no matter how much or how little influence you have over those laws and how they are made, no matter how those laws are enforced and no matter what interests or values those laws encourage or protect, then you can rest easy because you will always have, as the old country song goes, "a satisfied mind."

If you do not have a "satisfied mind" and you do not believe that the law of the land is "our law," if you have come to the conclusion that it is *their law*...

...then you have exiled yourself to their útangarðr.

You have wandered outside the enclosure, into the wild unknown. Their law is backed by the golden standard of violence, but the moral legitimacy of their law — especially the law of modern "democratic" governments — relies on the illusion that their law is vár lög, a product of communal consensus. To deny this illusion is heretical. It is a thoughtcrime.

Committing this thoughtcrime makes you a moral criminal. By refusing to acknowledge the moral legitimacy of the law, you make yourself a force of entropy that undermines their order. Even if you tell no one and take no action, you have spiritually taken the forest passage and become an element of insurgency. You have made war on the community in your heart.

"He who breaks the law has gone to war with the community; the community goes to war with him."

If you choose to make war on the community, you should expect the community make war upon you.

If you reject the Empire of Nothing, its laws and its values, if you curse and condemn The Empire, its agents and everything it represents — the Empire and its citizens in spirit will eventually curse and condemn you.

You will be regarded as untrustworthy, and rightfully so. Why would anyone trust anyone who openly rejected their values and renounced membership in their group. After all, you have made yourself a traitor...*to them.* That doesn't make you incapable of loyalty, and you may well be more loyal than those whose "loyalty" is merely a mask for fear of social and legal reprisal. But it is human nature to dehumanize outsiders and potential enemies. Citizens of the Empire, even with their carefully cultivated universal morality, will use that moral gear shift to dismiss your humanity — they will have no tears for you — if you break their law or challenge that universal morality. How many of these people really care what happens to a man after he's been declared a criminal, a terrorist, a racist, a sexist, a gang member, a cult member, or some other kind of separatist or "extremist?" The average person will wash their hands of him completely. And the sheepdogs — or wolves — of the Empire will feel like heroes for hunting him down and slaying him like a wild beast.

By committing yourself completely to a tribal group, others will become outsiders to you, and you will become an outsider to them. To become a barbarian is to live outside the boundaries of the Empire's laws and morality. They will call you an outlaw, a criminal, a "bad guy." You will become a wolf to them. You must be willing to accept that, and wear the head of the wolf proudly and defiantly. You will be a wolf to them because you are a wolf for your people, your pack, your tribe.

When they call you a beast, a monster, an outlaw, a parasite, a criminal, a "bad guy," remember that they are outsiders. They are strangers. You owe them no tears, no apologies, no excuses and no explanations.

Not my people, not my problem.

GINNUNGAGAP

In Norse lore, before the time of gods or men, there was a world of fire and a world of ice. Between the volcanic Muspelheim, and the glacial Niflheim, there was a mystical emptiness — a yawning nothingness known as *Ginnungagap*. Sparks vaulting forth from the neverending conflagration collided with the crystalline overflow of icy white rime, causing a vaporous reaction from which the giant Ymir emerged. Ymir drank the milk of a cosmic cow and eventually his enormity produced the progenitors of all giants. As Ymir fed from the cow Auðhumla, she licked a block of salty ice, revealing the shape Búri, forefather of the gods.

Búri sired a son named Borr, and Borr fathered three sons who are known as Odin, Vili and Vé.

Odin and his brothers murdered Ymir and made the world from his corpse. From the death of this colossus, they recycled death to create organic life, and brought order forth from the chaos of nothingness.

———————

As the overextended Roman Empire showed signs of weakness and exhaustion, tribes of non-Romans — barbarians — picked away at its rotting corpse. They looted, pillaged and plundered the great cities of the Empire for anything that seemed useful or appealing. By scavenging its remains, they survived, prospered, evolved and eventually coalesced into new nations. These nations rose to power, and havens of barbarism like Britain, France, Germany and Spain grew into centers of culture that sent their own imperial armies to conquer, convert and assimilate people in territories all around the world.

Now, these Empires have also become exhausted. Their once proud peoples have abandoned their ancestors and been taught to be ashamed of their histories. The old Empires have become rootless and formless. They move without direction, rolling over land and sea to entangle and adulterate each other in a brotherless world wedded to whoredom. The dissolution of difference and identity has become the one true religion of this new Empire of Nothing — this is their only dream for the future, their only final end, their heaven, their catholic caliphate of consumerism.

The choice available to us is to embrace this dream of the dying, to let go and become men of the Empire and follow it into emptiness — or to become the new barbarians, the forefathers of future Empires, who fight and flourish around the dying giant as we build new worlds from its remains.

Over the past century, as men came to grips with the decline of the West, their reaction has been one of hopelessness and despair. The word "occidental" is actually derived from a Latin root that means "to fall" as the sun falls in the West, and this Western sunset was always inevitable. While some sense of loss is understandable, ultimately this occidental melancholy is a testament only to lack of energy and imagination.

Our ancestors were born into tribes. They inherited their allies, their cultures, their traditions, their homelands. The forces of globalism may have destroyed connections to blood and soil, but they offer an unprecedented opportunity for barbarians to connect with like-minded men and women all around the world. Men of vision can beacon to each other across the grassless desolation of the Empire and travel its vast networks to come together, tear apart the remains of the old world and become forces of creation.

The Empire of Nothing has created an emptiness where anything can happen, where magic and creation can happen — a new Ginnungagap.

If you found yourself in the void with your brothers before the monstrous body of a dead god, what kind of world would you build from his corpse?

ACKNOWLEDGEMENTS

The original concept for this book was partially inspired by conversations I was having a few years ago with some friends who were in the military — specifically Max and Mike, among others. Mike Mathers has since become an important part of my own circle and I look forward to "planting trees of liberty" with him over the years here in Cascadia with The Wolves.

I would like to thank *my people* — my "*we*" — The Wolves of Vinland for accepting me as one of their own. Prospecting for and oathing into The Wolves has been a powerful and life-changing experience for me, and many of the "changes of the mind" I discuss in this book are changes I had to make to my own mind to make that process possible. I learn more about being a member of a tribe every day from The Wolves. Thank you especially to my brothers Paul and Matthias Waggoner for rolling the dice with me.

Following the success of *The Way of Men*, I've collected (or been collected by) a bunch of "guys" — as in, "Yeah, I know a guy for that." I have my gun guy, Greg Hamilton, who offered to train me and who kicks around ideas with me. I have my strength guy, Chris Duffin, who "shares vision" with me almost every day, and who constantly inspires me to do better and push harder at everything from training to business. I've got my obscure information guys, Trevor Blake and Michael Lopushok, who both read this manuscript and offered their thoughts. I've got my "renaissance strategist" guy, who like Odin has many names, but he is best known for his *mountain guerrilla* blog, his rifle courses and his book *The Reluctant Partisan.* Along with Justin Garcia — one of my MMA guys — from *The Pressure Project*, the three of us are writing about many of the same ideas from different angles. You can have all of the skill in the world, but eventually everything is about tribe and identity. All of these "guys," and probably many more, have contributed to development this book in some way or other.

I'd also like to thank Richard Spencer, who invited me to speak at two of his NPI conferences, where I sketched out some of the ideas in this book in the speeches "Becoming the New Barbarians," and "The Tribal Mind" — both of which you can currently watch on Spencer's RADIX/NPI YouTube Channel. Spencer has always backed me up, and believed I had something important to say, even though he catches a lot of shit from the autistic weirdos an nerd-virgins on the very far right for doing so.

Finally, I'd like to thank my readers. This book may be challenging and I may alienate some of you, but generally speaking I have some of the most humblingly strong, competent and courageous readers in the world. It's been extremely gratifying to have accomplished martial artists, athletes and military professionals read my work and confirm that my theories work in practice. It has also been inspiring to see other men, regular guys like me, realize there is something wrong with the modern world take steps to become the kind of men they want to be instead of settling for what is passable in The Empire of Nothing.

OTHER BOOKS
BY JACK DONOVAN

A Sky Without Eagles (2014)

The Way of Men (2012)

Blood-Brotherhood &
Other Rites of Male Alliance (2010)

Androphilia (2007)

FOR UPDATES
AND NEW WORK

www.jack-donovan.com

DISSONANT HUM

CASCADIA

CPSIA information can be obtained
at www.ICGtesting.com
Printed in the USA
BVOW08s0712140817
491735BV00003B/16/P